MW00774201

Faculty Development:

A Resource Collection for Academic Leaders

MAGNA

Madison, Wisconsin

Magna Publications
2718 Dryden Drive
Madison, WI 53704
Magnapubs.com

Copyright © 2018 by Magna Publications.

The articles in this book have been previously published in *Academic Leader, Distance Education Report,* and *The Teaching Professor* newsletters or have been adapted from Magna 20-Minute Mentor presentations.

ISBN: 978-0-912150-66-6

All rights reserved. Published 2018. It is unlawful to duplicate, transfer, or transmit this book in any manner without permission from the publisher.

Contents

Foreword.. 5

Chapter 1: Getting Started **9**

Making Faculty Development an Institutional Value and a
Professional Practice.. 10

Professional Faculty Development: The Necessary Fourth Leg........... 14

Faculty Development: A Model from Johns Hopkins........................ 16

A Theory of Faculty Development for Blended Learning 20

The Importance of Collective Leadership: Building and
Maintaining High-Performing Teams................................... 24

Does Online Faculty Development Really Matter?........................ 30

Open Educational Resources: An Easy Way to Enrich Faculty
Development 34

Chapter 2: Assessment and Evaluation **39**

Promoting a Culture of Assessment..................................... 40

Using Faculty Learning Communities to Support Program-Level
Assessment 44

Enhancing a Valuable Asset: Positives of
Thoughtful Staff Management.. 47

The Research Process and Its Relevance to the Culture of Assessment 52

Using Formal Program Review for Continuous Improvement............ 55

Preparing and Using Classroom Observations in
Faculty Teaching Evaluations.. 59

Is It Worth Revisiting Faculty Evaluation? 63

Teacher and Peer Assessments: A Comparison 67

Putting Assessment in Its Place.. 70

Chapter 3: Mentoring..**75**

Creating an Effective Mentoring Program 76

Design Considerations 78

Steps to Building an Effective Program 81

Mentorship Dos and Don'ts 82

Mentee Dos and Don'ts.. 85

Mentoring Program Guidelines and Tips............................. 87

Developing a Culture of Mentoring Excellence 89

Helping Faculty Develop a Scholarship Agenda 92

Using Academic Retreats to Enhance Academic Affairs Performance.. 96

Speed Mentoring.. 99

Chapter 4: Development Across Faculty Careers.............................**103**

   Making Changes: How Faculty Do It 104

   From a Teaching Assistant to a Teaching Professor 107

   How Can I Engage Adjunct Online Faculty in Professional
      Development? 110

   Adjunct Professional Development Improves Teaching, Builds
      Community 118

   Strategic HR Approaches to Building and Sustaining a
      Diverse Adjunct Workforce... 121

   Faculty Fellows Program Provides Incentives, Structure to Improve
      Teaching... 125

   Team Teaching: Active Learning Practice
      for Teachers 128

   After Promotion and Tenure Maintaining Faculty's Upward Trajectory
      130

   Encouraging Faculty Leadership Development................................. 134

   Best Practices in Preparing Academic Leaders.................................. 137

About the Contributors **140**

Additional Resources **145**

FOREWORD

Academia is one of a handful of professions in which it is the norm to hire new employees and then promote them to positions of leadership and greater responsibility with limited advance notice and little to no purposeful preparation or training.

This status quo is partially a result of a widespread feeling that "It's always been done this way, why change?" For whatever reason, as a career field, we seem to believe that newly hired faculty and recently promoted academic leaders will somehow intuitively "figure it out" and get it right. As a result, faculty and leaders continue to repeat many of the same mistakes that were made by their predecessors. Bumps, bruises, and missteps received in the School of Hard Knocks can be powerful teaching tools, but we can do better to teach faculty and leaders what is expected of them.

This repeating cycle of trial-and-error learning reminds me of an orientation activity that I witnessed as a faculty member at the United States Military Academy in New York. Each summer on R-Day (Reception Day), when students—new cadets in Military Academy parlance—arrive at West Point, they experience a longstanding tradition called "Step Up to My Line." Over the decades, it has played out in assorted ways, but the basic elements of the drama have remained the same.

Upper-class students, called Cadets in the Red Sash because of the large belt-like sashes they wear on R-Day, have earlier placed a line, usually made of duct or masking tape, on the ground approximately one foot in front of where they are standing. New cadets stand in front of a Cadet in the Red Sash with their backs turned to them. The Cadet in the Red Sash will direct a new cadet to "About Face" (which is military-speak for "turn around") and approach them.

The Cadet in the Red Sash loudly and crisply instructs the new cadet to "Step up to my line—not on my line, not over my line, not behind my line! Step up to my line!" The new cadet must approach the Cadet in the Red

Sash with their head and eyes locked in a straightforward position. If they glance down for any reason, they can be declared a failure and sent to the back of the line with instructions to try again in a few minutes. Unable to see the line on the ground, each new cadet must guess where it is and when they should stop, salute, and report to the Cadet in the Red Sash.

The point of this little exercise is that no matter what a new cadet does, they can be criticized. If a new cadet stops short of the taped line, the Cadet in the Red Sash can yell at them, "Did I not tell you to step *up* to my line and not *behind* my line? Go to the back of the line and try again!" Likewise, if a new cadet steps *over* the line, they can receive a similar negative evaluation. On the unlikely chance that a new cadet actually stops squarely on the line, the Cadet in the Red Sash can still yell at them, "Did I not tell you to step *up* to my line and not *on* my line? Go to the back of the line and try again!" This "Step Up to My Line" experience can repeat until either the Cadet in the Red Sash grows tired of the game or the new cadet chooses to quit and leave the Academy.

Sometimes I wonder if institutionally we don't orchestrate "Step Up to My Line" experiences for our faculty—especially in the first years after being hired as they run the gauntlet attempting to earn tenure. We can do the same thing to new academic leaders, as well, as they struggle to simultaneously learn budgeting skills, resource allocation, management, counseling, and the host of other tasks they're called upon to complete, but have seldom been trained to do.

Isn't it time to break this cycle and start doing better?

This book, I think, is a step in the right direction. These articles, which are written by a variety of qualified authors, have been assembled from *Academic Leader, Distance Education Report,* and Magna's 20-Minute Mentors to provide leaders in higher education—deans, department chairs, provosts, faculty developers, and others—with a guide for effective faculty development.

This book is organized into four sections: Getting Started, Assessment and Evaluation, Mentoring, and Development Across Faculty Careers. Briefly, here's what you can expect from each part: *Getting Started* makes a clear and convincing case for the importance and necessity of creating, funding, and supporting a meaningful faculty development program. *Assessment and Evaluation* provides ideas and possible ways that faculty performance can be meaningfully and constructively evaluated. The *Mentoring* section walks readers through creating and implementing a sustainable faculty mentoring program and includes a number of checklists, suggestions, and questions for program administrators, mentors, and mentees. The final section, *Development Across Faculty Careers*, discusses various ways to help your organization develop the next generation of academic leaders.

In short, this book includes a wealth of proven faculty development suggestions, tips, and ideas that are practical, specific, applicable in a wide range of academic settings, and most importantly, do-able. The skills and essential tools outlined here can be used to break the cycle of requiring faculty and leaders to "Step Up to My Line."

Kenneth L. Alford, Ph.D.
Brigham Young University
Colonel, U.S. Army (Ret.)

CHAPTER 1

•

Getting Started

Making Faculty Development an Institutional Value and a Professional Practice

Henry W. Smorynski, PhD

Sometimes faculty development programs are inherited by an academic leader, and other times they have to be built. In either case the academic leader needs to heed some wisdom from the Chinese classic the *Tao Te Ching.* Faculty development is a long journey wherever one starts; like a journey of 1,000 miles, it begins with the first step. Faculty development is also to be understood as a destination. Only if one has a clearly identified end for it will it achieve its desired destination—a highly effective and participatory faculty.

Faculty development program success begins with recruiting faculty to a specific institution's mission during the recruitment and interview process. Bringing faculty into an institution who are not committed to its teaching, research, and service mission incentives and imperatives will lead to mismatches between faculty career aspirations and institutional resource commitments. Such mismatches undermine collegiality and undercut faculty development efforts. Hiring faculty who are overly focused on their discipline versus teaching and the school's mission will lead to faculty dissatisfaction and turnover, with negative consequences for the classroom and within academic departments.

Beyond successful hiring, faculty programs will founder if they do not have a strong advocate at the highest level of academic administration. If the academic leader does not acquire and distribute resources consistent with the mission of the institution, wrong messages are sent. Faculty can become committed to one specific type of educational innovation. They can seek release time for their own career interests rather than the mutual interests of the institution and the faculty member. And they will come to view faculty development more as a competition for resources or an activity undervalued by the institution. Only strong academic administration leadership can provide the direction and energy necessary for a high-quality faculty development program. No faculty development director or coordinator, or even a faculty development resource office, can make up for the lack of a clear, constant, and resource-committed academic leader who visibly promotes and rewards effectively institutional mission-inspired faculty development.

A third key ingredient in faculty development success is choosing the right point person to be the daily spokesperson. Improper selection of the faculty development coordinator or director can sink any program. One needs to avoid the error of choosing the most innovative faculty member in the college or university. One should also not choose a faculty member well known for a particular kind of teaching, like case studies or computer simulations. The selection of the faculty development director or coordinator should be driven both by his or her commitment to all kinds of development and experimentation in teaching and research and by widespread colleague acceptance and confidence. Only a few faculty in any institution will meet both these criteria. Without both characteristics being present in the faculty development coordinator or director, the overall faculty development program and faculty participation in it will be limited to only highly motivated faculty or select faculty departments. It will never gain large-scale participation rates (over 75 percent). It will not reflect the necessary vitality to change and innovate as theories, methods, and research in higher education change regarding best practices.

A fourth element of a successful faculty development program involves the creation of a common basis for development efforts shared by the faculty as a whole. Although not widely accepted or understood by faculties in general, the work of L. Dee Fink can be very beneficial in creating that basis. His concepts articulated in *Creating Significant Learning Experiences: An Integrated Approach to Designing College Courses* can provide a common basis for faculty across all disciplines. By creating courses through a learner-centered approach versus a subject-oriented approach, one opens up the faculty to innovation, experimentation, and good teaching practice sharing, which are all vital to a healthy faculty development program. His model of an integrated course design brings together four key elements—learning situational factors, learning goals, teaching and learning activities, and feedback and assessment—into a powerful combination through the idea of "backward course design." This means the syllabus and course are designed from student learning objectives and not subject matter coverage.

If one has built these four elements into a faculty development program, then one needs to complement them with an anchoring and reinforcing faculty performance evaluation system. Tenure, promotion, and merit pay, where applicable, must identify faculty development as a key measurement for the evaluation and rewarding of faculty. A lack of consistency between academic leader messaging and promotion and tenure criteria used in any institution will doom any faculty development program to be engaged in primarily by true believers or innovative academic departments. It will not impact more than 25 to 40 percent of the teaching faculty, in my experience of promoting faculty development at nine different higher education institutions over 20 years. It will have very limited positive impact on teaching in the classroom, student retention, and institutional attractiveness and reputation.

Parker Palmer's book *Courage to Teach* should be required reading along with Fink's integrated course design. Palmer addresses clearly and convincingly the importance of individual faculty integrity to the teaching-learning process as being rooted in the integration of subject matter, student characteristics, and the faculty member's core identity as an educator. All three of these aspects must be visible and practiced in a widely appealing and engaging faculty development program.

Faculty development must be viewed as a diffusion process. If the fundamentals for success are put into place and practiced consistently, then the faculty development program will be successful both in terms of institutional impact and faculty career satisfaction. Building that diffusion effort systematically requires certain identified practices. These practices include a program that covers annually the wide-ranging interests of faculty that include teaching best practices, research time releases, team-teaching opportunities, faculty seminars and luncheons to share experiences led by colleagues, and annual visits by outside leaders in innovation in higher education. Program mix is a crucial sustaining element of successful faculty development programs.

Diffusion also depends on the annual or semi-annual required faculty development days tied to an institution's mission. These days highlight current faculty creativity and innovation across all disciplines in the institution. They are an important time of bonding the institutional commitment to faculty development.

Finally, an effective and successful faculty development program depends on each individual department promoting disciplinary and teaching innovations relevant to their courses, students, and disciplines to reinforce the overall institutional program.

Faculty development programs can easily achieve 25 to 40 percent faculty involvement and participation. But only programs that are structured from recruitment to post-tenure review will deliver a comprehensive institutional mission benefit for all faculty and the students they serve.

Reprinted from *Academic Leader,* July 2015

Professional Faculty Development: The Necessary Fourth Leg

Alan Altany

The well-known three-legged stool of academic life—teaching, research, and service—has been assumed to cover the main responsibilities of faculty in academic communities. But is there a missing leg that would add strength and stability to the stool? I propose there is. It's professional faculty development, and I would also propose that faculty committed to teaching should be its most articulate advocates. Here's a list of the reasons why professional development plays a critical role in the ongoing growth of teachers. Professional development does support all aspects of academic careers, but understanding its importance to teaching is my emphasis here.

- Professional development promotes faculty responsibility for continuous, career-long growth based upon not only the trial and error of experience, but also theory, research, and professional collaboration with colleagues.

- The understanding of instructional concepts and teaching processes can be expanded and deepened via professional development.

- Good teaching is not just a "you have it or you don't" skill, nor is it an automatic companion of terminal, disciplinary degrees. It is an action, process, and way of thinking and as such it constitutes serious, complex intellectual work. It requires regular reflection and exposure to new ideas and information that are inherently a part of good professional development activities.

- Professional faculty development connects faculty across disciplines and career stages, serving to create a pedagogical community within the college or university.

- Professional development is not remedial or something only for those having problems, but should be an integral part of every faculty member's efforts to become more effective in the classroom.

- Although professional development has often been viewed as supplementary within the academy, it actually plays a central role in faculty motivation and vitality across their careers.

- Without professional development opportunities, faculty are often isolated and unaware of beneficial, innovative pedagogical approaches.

- "One who dares to teach must never cease to learn" (Dana): Professional development provides opportunities for faculty to learn about learning, about teaching, about students, and about themselves.

- Professional development should not be an optional or occasional activity. Regular participation in professional development activities should be an expectation for all teachers.

- Professional development is the conscience of the professional academic. It makes teachers aware of what they do, asks them why, and challenges them to continually do it better.

- Professional development strengthens the affective, intellectual, and social aspects of academic life. It improves the academic experience at institutions for teachers and students.

During these times of very tight budgets, activities central to the success of teachers may be targeted for cuts. Professional development opportunities should not fall into that category, and those committed to teaching should be prepared with a set of reasons why.

Reprinted from *The Teaching Professor,* June 2011

Faculty Development: A Model from Johns Hopkins

Jennifer Patterson Lorenzetti, MS

The Johns Hopkins University Engineering for Professionals program allows busy professionals to earn a master's degree or certificate program by studying online or through conveniently scheduled courses located around the Baltimore-Washington, D.C., area. With its first online classes offered in 2001, it initially faced the problem of how to train its online faculty, particularly those adjunct professors who had never previously taught online.

"We used to do six hours on a Friday and threw all the information at them at once," says Denille Williams, instructional designer at Johns Hopkins. The results of this data dump were less than ideal. "They came back a week later and remembered none of it," says Williams. This lead to instructional designers needing to work with adjunct faculty one-on-one to teach them the material they'd forgotten.

To remedy this, Johns Hopkins introduced two courses that online faculty could take to improve their ability to develop an online course and to be successful in its facilitation. In a Sloan-C presentation on the subject, Williams states the goals in developing the courses as follows:

1. Introduce [faculty to the] development process
2. Get them to start thinking about their change in roles
3. Introduce them to online pedagogy and best practices
4. Produce a draft of their first development deliverable

Secondarily, the courses were designed to "immerse [adjuncts] in the online environment" and to "let them see good course design."

Course One: "Developing an Online Course"

The first of the two courses is called "Developing an Online Course," or "DOC." Adjunct faculty enter this course in a cohort and complete the course over three weeks.

"Developing an Online Course" is comprised of eight modules:
1. Introduction
2. Online Course Components and Development Process
3. Planning and Designing Your Online Course
4. Writing Learning Objectives
5. Developing Instructional Content and Multimedia
6. Learning Activities in the Online Classroom
7. Assessing Student Learning Online
8. Review and Next Steps

Course objectives include teaching the instructor to:
- Describe the online course development process
- Identify the components of an online course
- Complete a course design matrix
- Explain the purpose of course and module learning objectives
- Write course and module learning objectives that clearly identify the expected learning outcomes
- Design learning activities and assessments that are aligned with stated course and module learning objectives
- Explain how the Quality Matters rubric is used in the design and development of [a] course
- Describe the online student experience from [the instructor's] experience participating in [the] course.

At the end of the course, faculty are expected to have completed a course design matrix that will help guide them as they develop the 14 modules that will make up their 14-week online course. The subsequent course development process is expected to take an average of 23 weeks.

"In going through the first course, the instructors can actually do their [course] development process online," says Williams.

Completion of the course is predictive of the instructor's ability to complete the course development process in a timely way. "Instructors who don't complete the course take two to three times as long to develop a plan, and the course may be off schedule."

Course Two: "Online Teaching Strategies"

The second course has only run for a few semesters, but it has already become a useful part of faculty training. Called "Online Teaching Strategies," or "OTS," this course attempts to teach instructors how to move from a face-to-face classroom situation to an online facilitation situation.

There are six modules.

1. Introduction
2. Establishing an Online Presence
3. Online Discussion Management and Facilitation
4. Feedback and Grading
5. Online Course Facilitation and Time Management
6. Review and Next Steps.

This course fills a gap that existed prior to its development. "We never touched on how to teach and facilitate online." This course addresses that need, with content aimed at helping instructors "ensure an innovative, engaging, and high-quality learning experience for the students."

Stated course objectives as defined on the course syllabus include helping the instructor learn to:

- Facilitate peer-to-peer and peer-to-instructor interactions in an online course environment
- Employ key techniques to establish [their] online presence
- Implement strategies to manage workload while teaching in an online course
- Identify various formative assessment approaches and apply different strategies for providing timely and meaningful student feedback
- Formulate a plan to best implement online teaching strategies into a course.

Both DOC and OTS include discussion, assignments, quizzes, and an expected course average in order for the participants to earn a certificate of completion.

Advice for others

Although the training courses have not yielded any hard quantitative data demonstrating their success, Williams has a lot of anecdotal evidence to support their efficacy.

First, as mentioned, completion of DOC correlates positively with ability of the instructor to complete the course development process in a timely manner. While planning on nearly half a year from inception of the DOC course to completion of course development is a challenging proposition, Williams notes that those who complete DOC are better prepared to handle this challenge, while those who don't complete it often stall during course development.

Second, those who complete OTS seem to be creating students who are more satisfied. "They have better course reviews," Williams says. "Students have generally been more positive."

Developing training courses for online faculty is an important concern for institutions that offer wholly or partially online programs. Williams suggests these institutions heed advice from her experience.

- First, "it's important to provide pedagogical training." In contrast to providing only technical training on how to administer and run the class, institutions should also provide training that helps faculty develop content and facilitate interaction and learning in the online environment. This is important because the online environment often requires a different approach to teaching and learning than the face-to-face classroom.
- Second, Williams cautions others to "be considerate of adjunct instructors' time." Much like the adult students they teach, the adjunct instructors are busy with other work and family commitments. They will be on the lookout for wasted time and activities that don't further their learning. "They will tell you if they're not getting value," Williams says.

Overall, the Johns Hopkins series of two courses for adjunct faculty appears successful in helping these instructors in the Engineering for Professionals program design and develop quality courses and deliver them in a way that is satisfying for busy students. It is an example of faculty development done right.

Reprinted from *Distance Education Report,* February 2014

A Theory of Faculty Development for Blended Learning

Jennifer Patterson Lorenzetti, MS

Providing faculty development opportunities for those who teach blended learning courses requires a great deal of planning at the system level.

"Institutional leaders [need to] approach strategic planning in a thoughtful way," says Peter Rennert-Ariev, associate professor of education specialties at Loyola University Maryland.

At the recent Online Learning Consortium Blended Learning Conference and Workshop 2015, he explained a theory of faculty development for blended learning that "work[s] backward from the mission" to "lay the foundation for an innovative and integrated institutional approach to faculty development."

Start with the mission

"It's important to have a strategy and think about the mission," Rennert-Ariev says. "Begin with the end in mind."

As Loyola is a Jesuit institution, it begins with a commitment to "Ignatian pedagogy." To explain that idea, Rennert-Ariev quotes an address by Peter-Hans Kolvenback, S.J., of Georgetown University, who stated:

The pursuit of each student's intellectual development to the full measure of God-given talents rightly remains a prominent goal of Jesuit education. Its aim, however, has never been simply to amass a store of information or preparation for a profession . . . the ultimate aim of Jesuit education is, rather, that full growth of the person which leads to action—action based on sound understanding and enlivened by contemplation, that urges students to self-discipline and initiative, to integrity and accuracy.

This sort of thought informs the way faculty are trained at Loyola.

"It's based on good teaching and learning theory [with a] cycle of teaching and reflection," Rennert-Ariev says. Faculty development becomes a "serious mission" as it aims to help instructors foster this kind of intellectual development in their students.

Loyola's faculty development focuses on "how to help faculty design and teach in blended contexts in ways that are embedded in our unique institutional mission," Rennert-Ariev notes. It does so by:

- "Focusing on deep, rigorous, and sustained interaction cultivated among students, between students and faculty, and between students and content," and
- "Changing the relationships of instructional time and space to make flexible the contexts of instruction in order to better 'meet students where they are.'"

To help faculty become better blended course instructors, Loyola offers a digital pedagogy fellowship, a two-week workshop that helps faculty "develop cutting edge digital skills." The workshop provides "support for faculty converting a course to hybrid or online as well [as being] for faculty interested in revising a course by more fully integrating web-based approaches using instructional technologies," he explains.

The participants focus on "developing a coherent course design and pedagogical approaches that increase communication and collaboration among students, integrate digitally recorded class sessions, and deepen student learning through a variety of 'web-based' innovations." The workshop includes panel discussions about "cultivating the Jesuit perspective," sessions on integrating digital video and audio content, using library and open source resources, and handling asynchronous communications.

According to Rennert-Ariev, a recent workshop included:

- The panel discussion mentioned above.
- Training on "develop[ing] advanced uses of [the] LMS (Moodle) to enhance communication, collaboration, sharing of content, and use of multimedia resources."
- Training on "develop[ing] strategies to facilitate interactive, synchronous virtual class meetings to generate active student participation by enhancing personalization, interaction, and student engagement."
- Practice "developing expertise in asynchronous strategies including text based forums and other multimedia discussion tools to prompt interaction through sharing of images, documents, and videos."

- Information on "integrating library resources to support students' information literacy, supporting research needs, and providing access to online and open resources."
- Practice "developing expertise producing and integrating digitally (video and audio) recorded presentations and podcasts."

A transformative model

All of this supports what Rennert-Ariev calls "a transformative model of development rather than a technical one." This transformative model encourages faculty to develop knowledge of content, technology, and pedagogy rather than simply measuring competency.

Rennert-Ariev compares a competency-based approach to faculty development with a transformative approach in four main areas. In the "image of the online teacher," the competency-based approach sees the instructor as a disempowered technician who performs rote tasks. In a transformative approach, the instructor is "empowered and engaged in intellectual work." This dimension is about "fostering an image of the faculty as empowered and engaged in intellectual work that requires careful deliberation."

When considering the knowledge base for online teaching, the competency-based approach emphasizes an atomistic and behavioral strategy "based on rules and propositions." The transformative approach emphasizes integration of knowledge. This dimension is about "having a view of the knowledge base for blended teaching as complex and requiring integration of technological, pedagogical, and content knowledge."

Within the "view of online teaching and assessment of teaching," the competency-based approach is teacher-centered and context-independent, focusing on "replication of effective practices." The transformative approach focuses on the learner and the content. This dimension emphasizes "having a view of blended teaching and assessment that focuses on learner-centered experiences requiring exercise of judgement."

Finally, the professional development practices for the two approaches are different as well. The competency-based approach is characterized by "use of standardized templates [and] established routines." The transformative approach uses simulations, cases and dilemmas, self-reflection, and autobiographical work to provide professional development opportunities. This final dimension talks about "offering professional development practices that foster critical reflection."

"The transformative approach is more long-lasting," says Rennert-Ariev.

While this transformative theory of faculty development for blended learning is currently in use at Loyola, Rennert-Ariev is considering how it might have a broader reach. He notes that there is a Jesuit digital network forming that will link institutions, and he's curious "how we find better ways of connecting."

"Our experience is pretty localized," he muses. "We're thinking about our obligation to collaborate with one another." "It's embodying connectivism. We look for ways to connect to other institutions," he says, calling this connectivism "the engine behind change."

Reprinted from *Distance Education Report,* August 2015

The Importance of Collective Leadership: Building and Maintaining High-Performing Teams

Barbara Kaufman, PhD

Today's presidents and chancellors are donning more hats than ever before to provide skilled, visionary leadership. Yet in a challenging academic environment in which financial and technological pressures are mounting and resources are scarce, achieving institutional goals alone can be overwhelming. Team support is essential to help communicate and reinforce the senior administrator's all-inclusive messages. This support becomes critical when initiatives such as reprioritizing resources and/or restructuring academic affairs are under consideration and when stakeholders are increasingly assertive. High-performing teams that go the extra mile to support and execute the leader's vision and priorities are needed to ensure successful implementation.

High-performing teams that additionally put aside interpersonal or philosophical differences and work for the common good of the university make the leader's objectives more attainable. Though difficult to build and even more challenging to sustain, these deeply committed teams are vital in this high-stakes environment.

Changing leadership environment

Administrative leadership roles are more complex and challenging today. Yet expectations remain high that campus and system leaders will handle both internal and external responsibilities with finesse and success. These areas may include but are not limited to board relationships, new public-private partnerships, crisis management, shared governance challenges, and fundraising that secures alternative sources of revenue. This demanding balancing act is further complicated by pressure from parents and legislators not to raise tuition. At the same time, increases in student loans are expected and state funding for public universities continues to shrink. In addition, the push to offer massive open online courses (MOOCs) is facing resistance from faculty who are concerned about the impact of MOOCs on the quality of education and on their job security. Twenty-first century students also expect a quality education that guarantees a job, increased accessibility to resources and professors, and schedule flexibility. As a result, leaders are faced with an insurmountable workload of strategic choices and decisions.

Benefits of a high-functioning team

Today's reality is that initiatives cannot be successful if they are driven solely by an individual chancellor or president. High-functioning teams are essential.

The most effective leadership teams go a step beyond successful implementation and speak with one voice in communicating a leader's vision and key priorities. Like a well-oiled machine, they work together to communicate the need for change and the rationale for decisions and to seek critical buy-ins from diverse constituent groups.

By allowing the president or chancellor to function more efficiently, high-performing teams contribute to propelling their institution forward. By leveraging their individual expertise, they help round out the strengths and weaknesses of the president's portfolio and present a strong collective leadership face to the campus community.

Challenges to building a high-performing team

Building and maintaining high-performing teams can be challenging. Individual style differences—such as a preference for collaboration versus a preference to be in charge, or an inability to move between divergent and convergent thinking—can create stumbling blocks to success. Here are just a few of these challenges:

1. **Conflicting sense of urgency that produces conflict among team members**. For example, a CFO might butt heads with a chief academic officer if they don't see eye to eye on how quickly to move ahead on an administrative restructuring.

2. **Individual style preferences prevent team members from recognizing the potential power that can be harnessed from their differences.** The cabinet member who processes quickly might have little patience with a colleague who prefers to table a decision until the next meeting. Nothing is accomplished or settled by resorting to playing the blame game.

3. **Resistance to change based on past assumptions harnessed to their differences.** Too often team members roll their success strategies forward from their prior role on a different campus or in a different sector rather than embracing their new campus culture.

4. **Reluctance to let go of assumptions and worldviews.** Entrenched in their own positions and ways of doing things, some team members may refuse to take advice from colleagues. Often this is intended to show others that they possess the leadership skills to do the job, but in fact this attitude makes collaboration next to impossible.

5. **Inconsistency on the president's part.** Unclear, conflicting, or mixed messages about decisions can erode team trust. Unsure what the president wants, team members may sabotage the decision, disengage, or resort to coping mechanisms, such as vying for the leader's attention. As a result, there is no sense of shared responsibility or accountability for outcomes.

Strategies for developing and maintaining high-performing teams

Campus communities and cultures vary widely, so no institutional goals are identical and no two teams are alike. Yet every team has the potential to be high-performing if leaders follow these critical paths to success:

- **Develop a successful onboarding process.** "You cannot assume high-performing individuals will automatically and independently become high-performing team members," says Michele Neal-on-Woods, PsyD, national president of the Chicago School of Professional Psychology. "Onboarding new senior administrators is an essential function of the CEO and one that requires dedicated time, careful planning, and the deliberate engagement of all members of the leadership team. When the CEO does not attend carefully to such onboarding, he or she opens up the team to not only unhealthy team dynamics but confusion in project and role execution." To onboard successfully, provide a shared understanding of campus governance; indicate how decisions are really made and by whom; and describe the campus, system, and state political environments. Then state clearly any and all expectations. In addition, develop and consistently use an effective mentoring process and/or buddy system.

- **Encourage team members to work together to accommodate differences.** Utilize an assessment tool to uncover individuals' preferred operating styles and preferred ways of achieving goals. Determine to what degree these preferences align with or conflict with the way the rest of their colleagues on the senior leadership team work. Encourage the sharing of individual expertise and strengths within the group to help balance out the president's portfolio.

- **Avoid solving issues between and among team members.** Encourage team members who are at odds with each other to work through their differences utilizing collaborative decision making and conflict management techniques. If there are clear and legitimate differences of opinion that cannot be resolved, only then, with both individuals in the room, should the leader serve as mediator.

- **Role-model collaboration across boundaries.** Communicate clear goals and responsibilities. Give and receive regular constructive feedback. Do not wait for the annual performance review. Give the team opportunities to make quick course corrections before bad habits take root and grow. High-functioning teams benefit from a shared understanding of role overlap across boundaries and the diversity of opinions.

- **Create an environment where "speaking truth to power" is encouraged.** Coined by the Quakers to address the issue of non-violent ways to deal with conflict, this term, in a broader sense, invites team members to be candid in discussions with one another and the leader in order to avoid groupthink. Honest dialogue permits the exchange of vital information and innovative ideas crucial in the development and maintenance of high-functioning teams. Address key questions openly to provide a better sense of team ownership, role clarity, and challenges on the horizon. This will lay the groundwork for future success. For example, following a challenging discussion, immediately develop a few talking points before everyone walks out the door. This will test the degree to which the team is on the same page and their ability to communicate decisions with fidelity.

- **Help new team members recognize that their new role may be very different from the one they held at their former campus.** This can be a difficult adjustment, especially for those who held a similar position for decades or who have worked in diverse environments. Don't let assumptions about what the leader expects go unstated.

- **Demonstrate consistent behavior.** It is important for leaders to send consistent messages and to avoid even the appearance of flip-flopping in decision making. If there is new information that impacts a prior decision, say so. Then provide a context for changing the decision in a face-to-face meeting; emails can be misinterpreted. Follow up on commitments, and role-model the behavior expected of others.

- **Create a sense of not only individual but also shared accountability.** To avoid sending a mixed message about what behavior will be rewarded, ensure that performance management processes assess both individual and team contributions.

- **Keep in mind that succession is inevitable.** More often than not, team members will leave. Whether this is the result of career aspirations, retirement, or job relocation, they will need to be replaced. "A president should presume that even if they have selected all of their direct reports, the cabinet will have a shelf life ranging from three to seven years," says Mohammad H. Qayoumi, president of San Jose State University. "Even in those unusual circumstances when a cabinet remains together for the above duration, the president must seek ways to invigorate the team with new and audacious goals and directions so the team can rejuvenate and transmute itself. Otherwise, the cabinet will experience boredom, monotony, and disengagement that lead to a dysfunctional team. Therefore, recognizing the shelf life of a cabinet can help a president to always maintain a high-performing team."

Turning vision into reality

In higher education, no matter how dynamic the individual administrative leader may be, a skilled senior leadership team that thrives in complex and less predictable environments is essential for achieving institutional goals. As the arc of leadership continues to evolve, team accountability and effectiveness are vital to the future of each institution. Certainly, challenges exist, especially as the composition of the team changes over time. Yet considering the benefits gained, investing the time and effort into building and maintaining high-performance teams is a workable and effective game plan that will continue to move institutions forward.

Reprinted from *Academic Leader,* September 2013

Does Online Faculty Development Really Matter?

Jennifer Patterson Lorenzetti, MS

Laurence Boggess has had an interesting career path to his current position as the director of faculty development for the Penn State World Campus. After 25 years as a K-12 administrator, he earned his PhD at Penn State and continued on to take a faculty position in the department of educational leadership at Miami University. He moved to the college of education at Penn State before taking his current position as director. Along the way, he has formed his own opinions about the importance of online faculty development and whether it really matters.

Does it matter?

Boggess poses this question, then allows that "the follow-up question is, 'to whom?'" He explains that this question is a natural outgrowth of the understandable uncertainty that accompanies these sorts of training endeavors. "We always wonder, 'Is what I'm doing making a difference?'" he says. "Does it matter to the faculty and administration?"

Part of the question is how the success of a faculty development program will be measured. "What are the metrics we're going to use to measure student success? You can't draw a straight line from faculty [development] to student success; there are too many other factors," Boggess says. However, the question remains: "How can we convince the administration to [fund the program] and faculty to come take our courses? What are the metrics that are meaningful?" While he understands that many people aren't thinking of this ROI perspective on faculty development, he says that, in the current climate, "they will be."

Boggess explains the problem like this: "Increasingly, universities are suggesting or requiring some credential—a course or a series of courses or modules—to 'prepare' or 'qualify' faculty to teach online. However, there is a tenuous research thread, at best, associating faculty training and student learning. Given the inability of educational research to establish credible measures of causality, faculty developers and faculty development researchers commonly look to proxy measures of effectiveness…"

Instead of these proxy measures, Boggess proposes the collection of data that more closely measures the success of online faculty development.

Higher education will be looking at metrics to measure the success of online faculty development initiatives because online learning has matured in the higher education environment. "Nationally, we've accepted that online learning is here to stay," he says. Therefore, the notion of having intentional faculty development has also matured.

Success at the World Campus

Penn State World Campus offers a nationally-recognized series of courses for its online faculty. The initial course, OL 1000: Welcome to World Campus, is followed by courses on teaching the adult learner, teaching the military learner, accessibility online, and using the LMS. All of these courses are self-paced. Additional instructor-led, cohort courses are also available.

The core course, OL 2000: Effective Online Instruction, makes up part of the online teaching certificate that instructors can earn. This four-week, instructor-led, cohort class teaches competencies in pedagogy, management, and technology. To date, nearly 1,400 individuals have taken the course, including faculty, instructional designers, staff, administrators, and graduate students. Completion of this certificate demonstrates that "faculty have taken their interest in online teaching seriously," Boggess says.

To demonstrate the effectiveness of this course, Penn State undertook a study of faculty self-reports in the course evaluation of OL 2000. The study sought to show how faculty experienced the course and their assessment of its outcomes. This study was conducted via a quantitative analysis of the faculty responses on the written portion of the course evaluation. More than 250 individual faculty members contributed written responses that could be included in the study, which covered 22 sections of the class from 2012-2015.

Three major findings resulted. In a recent Online Learning Consortium conference presentation, Boggess summarized these findings as follows:

- A significant majority had positive experiences.
- Their pre-course concerns were affective and technical.
- Their post-course reflections highlighted relief expressed as increased comfort, competence, and confidence.

In other words, the course made the majority of faculty feel much better about their ability to teach online.

Many faculty members went into the course with significant anxiety, signaled by words like "unprepared," "incompetent," "inexperienced," "uncomfortable," and even "lonely." However, when asked to describe their feelings post-course, the words used signaled a sense of relief: "surprised," "comfortable," "confident," and "competent" were all used.

The new level of comfort seems to have been brought about by certain faculty discoveries that helped them feel better prepared.

Boggess explains that the faculty discovered, among other things:

- Resources they didn't know existed.
- Colleagues of mix[ed] experience.
- Techniques for engagement.
- Techniques for student motivation.
- Strategies for personalizing a course.
- Strategies for time management.

Although there were no hard data connecting the completion of the course with student success, the results of the course were quite clear. "Faculty come [to the course] with an overwhelming feeling of apprehension that translates to a feeling of relief," Boggess says. "I think that's a good finding to share with administration," he says, explaining that this information can have a great deal of power when disseminated throughout the university. Faculty tell other faculty that they needed to do the training,"
he says.

The value of the online faculty training has indeed spread through the university. The institution has undertaken a pilot program for graduate students that allows these new instructors to learn some of the skills they will need in the classroom, and the response has been tremendous. "We combined a couple of courses [and] use the badge system to microcredential it," he says. The institution expected about 30 graduate students to sign up for the training, and some 350 did so. To date, about 280 have completed the training. "A strong motive was [that they] wanted to have some credential on their CV," he noted. This indicates a desire to demonstrate the commitment to online teaching also seen among the non-student faculty. "We want to start following them longitudinally," Boggess says. However, at this time, the graduate student training is open online to Penn State graduate students, with discussions still ongoing about whether this training could be opened to graduate students across the country.

When asked about his advice for other institutions thinking about a Penn State-style online faculty development program, Boggess urges his peers to think about things in terms of impact. "If you're not thinking about metrics, you should be," he says.

"Faculty development is assumed to be good, [but that thinking's] probably not enough anymore." Instead, institutions should take charge of their online faculty development and how it is perceived by faculty, administration, and other constituents.

"We're in control of the message at this point," Boggess says.

Whether institutions like Penn State can keep in control requires forward thinking and a desire to demonstrate the effectiveness of training.

Reprinted from *Academic Leader,* January 2016

Open Educational Resources: An Easy Way to Enrich Faculty Development

Jennifer Patterson Lorenzetti, MS

Open educational resources (OER) have gained recognition for their use in developing student-facing courses, but their usefulness goes much further. OER can also be extremely helpful in creating faculty development courses, contends Kelvin Thompson, EdD, associate director of the University of Central Florida Center for Distributed Learning.

Using these resources, however, starts with understanding them.

Fair use of OER

An OER is "a resource to support the curation of effective pedagogical practices in online and blended courses," Thompson says. "Like OER in credit-bearing courses, OER as a rejuvenating factor [in faculty development] can be powerful."

Using OER effectively begins with understanding the power that comes with the Creative Commons licensing that typically governs such materials. In many cases, an instructional designer might link to intellectual property that they don't have permission to repurpose or copy to a local site as a way of protecting the original copyright holder while making the information available to a course or user. Linking to desired information rather than hosting it locally is a technique that is typically used to respect the original copyright holder.

But links quickly break, leaving the desired material abandoned in cyberspace. And Creative Commons licensing allows for much broader use.

Under Creative Commons licensing, a user can download a piece of intellectual property and host it locally, ensuring that it remains available as long as is needed. "You can download it and host it on your own server," Thompson says, emphasizing the control that Creative Commons licensing gives the user.

Even more powerful, Creative Commons licensing allows users to "remix" the content, adapting it to their own needs. Rather than "reinventing the wheel," starting with Creative Commons-based resources allows the user to recreate another user's work on information or problems held in common, then make additions, subtractions, and edits that will customize the work to the new user's individual context.

For example, Thompson tells of one user who reported hearing that she was charged with getting 200 faculty members ready to teach online by the following fall term. With a bit of judicious Google searching, she found the UCF BlendKit information (*http://blended.online.ucf.edu/*), and "it gave her a place to start," Thompson says. A look at the model courses could well have given her and her faculty a good start in developing a new online course.

It's easy to share

"It's scary at first to share" information through Creative Commons licensing, Thompson acknowledges. But he says that getting over the anxiety of that first time can be a good step toward sharing information and resources that may be useful to others. "An instructional designer has an internal document or checklist and gets a request to share. They put a Creative Commons license on it, and they see the world didn't end."

Thompson urges other educators to share their work via Creative Commons license. "Make it public and make it accessible. There's no registry; you just do it," he says.

Creators also don't need to be afraid that sharing information and resources means completely losing control. Thompson notes that Creative Commons makes available a "chooser" (*https://creativecommons.org/choose/*) that helps users decide which aspects of their work they wish to share. Users of this tool can input whether they would like to allow adaptations of the work to be shared and if they wish to allow their work to be shared commercially.

"Open doesn't necessarily mean free. You can charge and make it a non-commercial license," Thompson says.

Creative Commons licenses range from a public domain dedication, the most open option, to a license requiring attribution and disallowing both non-commercial and derivative work, the least open. "Creative Commons really puts you in the driver's seat; it makes it clear how you want people to use [your work]," Thompson says.

The tool then selects the appropriate Creative Commons license and suggests the appropriate graphics to accompany the work. The tool also will suggest machine-readable metadata and HTML code that allows the work to be more easily found with a search engine.

Remixing

All of this leads to the true power of Creative Commons licensing: remixing. Users can take the licensed material and use it in new ways to suit their own needs. Users just need to attribute the original work appropriately and according to the Creative Commons license used.

Some examples of appropriate attribution from Creative Commons' extensive FAQ (*http://wiki.creativecommons.org/FAQ*) include:

- CC licenses allow for flexibility in the way credit is provided depending on the medium, means, and context in which a licensee is redistributing licensed material. For example, providing attribution to the creator when using licensed material in a blog post may be different than doing so in a video remix.
- If you change the terms and conditions of any Creative Commons license, you must no longer call, label, or describe the license as a "Creative Commons" or "CC" license, nor can you use the Creative Commons logos, buttons, or other trademarks in connection with the modified license or your materials.
- You may always choose to waive some license terms or conditions. Material licensed under a CC license but with additional permissions granted or conditions waived may be compatibly licensed with other material under the same license.

(More information is included at the website above.)

OER can be a boon for those who wish to provide robust faculty development opportunities. They allow developers to source the best of university practices, with the expectation that, under Creative Commons licensing, the resulting products will be shared with others. This is why Thompson calls OER "like watering holes on an African savannah."

Resources for Faculty Development

UCF Resources
- BlendKit Course - *http://blended.online.ucf.edu/blendkit-course/*
- TOPR - *http://online.ucf.edu/teach-online/resources/teaching-online-pedagogical-repository-topr/*
- Faculty Seminars in Online Teaching - *http://online.ucf.edu/teach-online/professional-development/faculty-seminars/*
- TOPcast: The Teaching Online Podcast - *http://online.ucf.edu/teach-online/professional-development/topcast/*
- Faculty Multimedia Workshop Series - *http://online.ucf.edu/teach-online/professional-development/faculty-multimedia-workshop-series/*
- IDL6543 Diigo pages - *https://www.diigo.com/outliner/6s78up/IDL6543-Bookmarks?key=ncyouebj34*
- Teach - *http://online.ucf.edu/teach-online/*

Other Institutions
- Open SUNY - *http://commons.suny.edu/opensuny/*
- Oregon State OSU - Online Education Trends - *http://ecampus.oregonstate.edu/online-education-trends/articles/128/*
- San Diego State University - *https://sdsu-cdi.wikispaces.com/Faculty+Development+Program+Design*
- PennState - Online Resources *https://weblearning.psu.edu/resources/penn-state-online-resources/*

Collections
- Merlot - *http://facultydevelopment.merlot.org/*

Organizations
- OLC - *http://onlinelearningconsortium.org/*
- EDUCAUSE/ELI - *http://www.educause.edu/eli*
- WCET/WICHE - *http://wcet.wiche.edu/*

Reprinted from *Distance Education Report,* November 2015

CHAPTER 2
•
Assessment and Evaluation

Promoting a Culture of Assessment

Rob Kelly

Many people often view assessment as a laborious burden, something that serves no other good purpose than accreditation obligations. Building a culture of assessment can help faculty see its value for continuous improvement and encourage them to participate in assessment efforts in meaningful ways.

In an interview with *Academic Leader*, Fang Du, director of assessment and program development at the University of Mount Union, discussed what a culture of assessment looks like and shared lessons learned at her institution.

According to Du, there are four hallmarks of a culture of assessment:

- **Higher learning first.** "Of course, every campus is about learning, but traditionally the indicators of that learning have been retention rates and graduation rates, the curriculum offered, and the accumulation of credits. But these are not what I would say are 'higher learning.' If the institution put higher learning first, all learning—regardless of discipline, general education, major, or minor—would be based on overall learning goals and competency. [In addition, learning] would incorporate high-impact practices, such as study abroad, experiential learning, internships, and writing-intensive courses. More important, higher learning is reflective, integrative, and lifelong," Du says.

- **Assessment as a prerequisite and central condition of that higher learning.** "Every teacher does assessment in the classroom, but that doesn't constitute a culture of assessment at the institution," Du says. Real assessment that is the central condition of higher learning has the following characteristics:

- Assessment plans are comprehensive policies at the program and institutional level.
- Assessment is outcome-based rather than input-based.
- Staff and faculty work together to contribute to program-level and institutional-level assessment. It's not an individual faculty effort.

- **Organizational structures that support assessment**. Mount Union has a faculty committee on assessment and uses the Academic Quality Improvement Program, a continuous quality improvement approach that is integrated into the institution's administrative structures. The university also has a policy for periodic program review, which requires annual reporting and a visit by an external reviewer every seven years.

- **Ongoing professional development opportunities for faculty and staff involved with assessment**. "Nurturing people in terms of assessment is very important. It's a discipline. It's a thing to learn. It's not that you get a PhD and you know how to do assessment. Professional development needs to be continuous," Du says.

For the past three years, Mount Union has offered five days of workshops in May (right after commencement), a time when faculty traditionally leave campus for the summer. Participation in these workshops are voluntary. In the first year, the dean gave each participating faculty a $500 stipend. Now, although the workshops are still voluntary, they are a prerequisite for teaching in the university's new Integrative Core.

When Du became assessment director in 2009, she worked with the assessment committee to change the program review process from a curriculum review and resource-counting process to one that is based on learning outcomes for each major and minor.

The assessment committee, which consists of six standing members, created a glossary of assessment terms and uses professional development workshops to help faculty understand the relationships among course-level, program-level, and institution-level assessment.

Another goal of ongoing professional development is to help faculty consider the uses and benefits of assessment beyond producing reports for accreditation. Du explains that assessment can help with continuous improvement, and that although assessment requires time and effort on the part of faculty, it actually reduces the amount of time and effort put into continuous improvement.

"Think of assessment as a means, not the end. So many people think assessment is the end. 'You asked me to do assessment. I did it. I'm done.' But no, assessment is only a means to help you achieve your end [continuous improvement]. In order to do that work efficiently, you have to embark on assessment," Du says.

Lessons learned

In her time as assessment director, Du has learned the following lessons (grouped by assessment culture hallmarks):

- **Higher learning**
  - Teaching content is not enough. Teaching habits of mind is more important.
  - Professors no longer stay in their discipline silos.
  - We need to have more discussions about pedagogy.
  - We should start to design key assignments/common rubrics together, not as individuals collecting artifacts, because they all take years.
- **Assessment as a prerequisite and central condition of learning**
  - Listening/understanding is important.
  - "Faculty allies are crucial. I found a few faculty leaders on campus and I started working with them one by one, which helped me bring that assessment 'song' to other people. I'm sure on each campus you can find several discipline leaders who have a deep understanding of how important assessment is. I have been very grateful for those faculty leaders who are willing to work with me in each stage. Once I have them, things become a little easier, because they're so respected on our campus," Du says.
- **Organizational structures**
  - "An effective assessment structure integrates administrative leadership and faculty governance bodies. You need administrative leadership and faculty and staff. Expertise is significant. You need to have someone who really has assessment expertise in general, not just assessment in biology or assessment in education, while you're beginning to establish that culture," Du says.
- **Professional development**
  - Take faculty morale into consideration during times of rapid change. When the University of Mount Union was building its

assessment culture, "people were frustrated. We almost asked them to do too much, to have a new curriculum and learn all things assessment. They had just redesigned every course they'd been teaching. It was a time of rapid change. We should have taken people's morale into consideration," Du says.

- There are emotional investments in assessment, technology, and curriculum.
- You can require a program/department to do things, but do not require individual faculty members to do anything.
- A new curriculum and its assessment does not have to be perfect, but it needs to have the capacity for continuous improvement.

Reprinted from *Academic Leader,* March 2015

Using Faculty Learning Communities to Support Program-Level Assessment

Rob Kelly

Faculty learning communities (FLCs) can be useful in addressing a wide variety of faculty development needs. The California State University System uses FLCs to address systemwide priorities, such as faculty leadership development, use of innovative pedagogies, and program-level assessment.

CSU uses a model based on the work of Milton Cox, engaging groups of up to 15 faculty members in a structured, yearlong experience with defined goals and required deliverables. When Wayne Tikkanen, director of the Institute for Teaching and Learning at CSU, put out a call for proposals to faculty development centers within the CSU system to develop ways to employ FLCs to meet institutional needs, several directors proposed using them for facilitating program-level assessment.

One of the advantages of the FLC approach to faculty development is the amount of time on task it provides. Amy Liu, director of California State University, Sacramento Office of Academic Program Assessment, facilitates FLCs on program-level assessment. "The faculty learning community gave us a longer time for faculty to really talk about why we're doing assessment," Liu says. Other faculty development efforts such as workshops and one-on-one consultation are typically short-term efforts that typically focus on how-to information. By offering yearlong FLCs, participants learn how to do program-level assessment as well as internalize why it's necessary, which is important because, as Liu says, "If faculty don't know why we're doing it, then they have all kinds of misconceptions and they're not going to be motivated to do it."

"Think of an FLC as a class for faculty," Tikkanen says, "where you have a curriculum [that] has readings and assignments—in our case, we refer to the latter as deliverables. When you design such a course, you want to make sure that the deliverables are things that will be used when [participants] are done with the FLC.

For example, if you're doing program-level assessment, one of the deliverables might be a set of outcomes for the program, an assessment instrument, or a rubric. These are items that they develop to put into use in the program. This is not make work. They see exactly what the work contributes to the FLC's goals, and they're being guided by facilitators who have content expertise and know how to keep the conversation going."

Participation in FLCs at CSU Sacramento is voluntary and open to all faculty; however, each program needs to have more than one representative. Liu has found that interested faculty members tend to come from departments that are under review or soon will be. This sense of urgency often provides the initial motivation.

Liu further helps motivate participants by reminding them that assessment is not an added duty; it's about improving student learning, something that is already part of what they do as faculty members. In addition, she reminds participants, "It's a learning process. You don't have to be perfect as long as you keep student learning and student success in mind."

One of the strengths of the FLC approach is that it brings together a diverse group, which, Tikkanen says, "will often give you the best solutions."

The facilitator's role is to focus the discussion. Liu typically limits the scope of the FLC to two or three learning outcomes common to all programs (e.g., critical thinking, written communication, information literacy). The goal is to get faculty to learn from each other through discussions about reading assignments and individual deliverables.

Each FLC has a detailed syllabus, but facilitators need to balance that structure with the needs of the faculty. "Some of them are not going to be as adept as others on certain topics," Tikkanen says. "[Facilitators] need to have some flexibility to be able to accommodate them and bring them up to speed with the rest of the group. Facilitators have to use dialogue protocols, so they can make sure the discussion involves all participants."

Trust is an important element of any FLC, and it can take some time for the group to develop a sense of community where participants feel free to express their opinions without feeling judged. Regular meetings over a long period help build community.

In addition to the tangible deliverables of the FLC, Liu wants to create assessment advocates and mentors. "Our hope is that through the faculty learning community, we change the culture of assessment on our campus," Liu says.

Tikkanen offers the following recommendations for using FLCs:

- **Prepare, but be flexible.** Have the curriculum fully mapped out even if you digress from it. "No battle plan survives contact with the enemy," says Tikkanen, quoting German military strategist Helmuth von Moltke. "But having a plan at least tells the faculty where you want to go."

- **Provide incentives.** Show faculty that you value their participation by providing incentives such as stipends.

- **Have FLC participants sign a contract.** Outline requirements and meeting times and dates. Defer paying development funding to participants until after they have completed their assignments.

- **Keep it confidential.** "The deliverables can be as public as you want them to be, but whatever happens in discussion should stay confidential," Tikkanen says. "This helps develop trust and helps faculty work better together."

- **Don't give up on faculty who aren't making progress.** "Sometimes it takes time for all the pieces to get sorted out," Tikkanen says.

- **Pace yourself.** Keep an eye on the big outcomes, and don't try to get everything accomplished in the first few meetings.

Reprinted from *Academic Leader,* November 2014

Enhancing a Valuable Asset: Positives of Thoughtful Staff Management

Jane Williams, PhD, and N. Douglas Lees, PhD

Formal reports and general discussions within the academy about depart-ment or school productivity focus almost exclusively on the work of the faculty. This accounts for the attention now being paid to the chairs' evalua-tions of faculty that target strategies designed to maintain high performance and, in some cases, to drive improvement. While it is difficult to argue that this approach is inappropriate, ask almost any chair how their department would fare without the support provided by their staff, and they will admit that virtually every aspect of the operation would be negatively impacted if they had less talented and motivated staff. Yet, in many departments, staff are not regularly evaluated at a depth comparable to faculty, if at all, and are rarely the recipients of opportunities to enhance and expand their skills.

Our different colleges have differing faculty-to-staff ratios and staff with varying levels of expertise. For example, a small undergraduate-only college may have departments with a faculty-to-staff ratio of 10 to 1 or higher. In some instances, a single staff member may be shared by two small depart-ments. In both cases, the individual must perform multiple tasks including placing orders through purchasing, appointing adjuncts, filing travel reim-bursements, fielding phone calls, greeting visitors, setting appointments, and so on. In larger institutions where research and graduate programming are prominent, faculty-to-staff ratios can be 1 to 1 or lower. The tasks at the small institution done by a single person are now accomplished by several individuals. In addition, there are graduate and undergraduate advisors;

graduate admissions personnel; pre-award and post-award grant personnel; development officers; IT personnel; outreach coordinators; and specialized technical help in science and engineering fields to maintain instrumentation, prep teaching labs, operate facilities such as animal rooms, core labs, greenhouses, fabrication labs, and collections; plus some more exotic staff such as instructional design experts, glass blowers, and carpenters. It is not difficult to imagine the chaos, productivity losses, and frustration that would take place if any one of most of these functions were done poorly.

Let us now return to the notion of staff evaluation (or management) in the context of the large, complex research university. Clearly, the chair could not and should not attempt to evaluate all the staff. In cases where there is a hierarchy of function among clusters of staff (e.g., a senior or chief accountant and several junior accountants), those at the higher end would evaluate the others. In other cases, faculty would perform this function. For example, the director of undergraduate studies would evaluate the undergraduate advisors while the director of graduate programs would evaluate the graduate advisors and those who work in the graduate admissions office. Delegation can work in these cases, but true equity in the process is achieved only when the evaluators develop comparable criteria, use the same evaluative language, and meet as a group to discuss the particulars of each case. Finally, there is the issue of chairs and their delegates in reviewing the work of those with high school diplomas to PhDs and in widely varying and non-disciplinary fields. For example, the chair of chemistry evaluates faculty on teaching, research, and service—but how does he or she formatively evaluate someone with an MBA (the senior accountant) and IT staff, all of whom have far more expertise in their areas than the chair? Perhaps this is one reason why in-depth reviews of staff performance are often "forgotten."

The overall goals of effective staff performance management include gathering data for promotion consideration and for merit pay. However, these administrative goals are overshadowed in importance by goals that are developmental and promote relationship building. Chairs and other supervisors will have the opportunity to provide feedback that reinforces, guides, and motivates future behavior. Development can be further enhanced by support for additional training or encouragement for new activities. By demonstrating genuine commitment in ensuring that individual staff have the opportunity for personal and professional growth through these developmental efforts, the supervisor can energize the staff member and establish long-term loyalty. Finally, regular face-to-face communication on job performance can contribute to building a high-trust relationship.

Effective performance management can lead to personal development and improvement in performance. It provides the opportunity to identify changes needed in the job description. It may also lead to identifying and acknowledging staff contributions that were previously overlooked, allowing the supervisor to identify individual aspirations and perhaps discover new talents from which the department may benefit. In situations where resources are scarce, it is an opportunity to express appreciation and provide recognition for the important work that the staff contribute to the mission of the department.

There are several criteria one could use to assess the effectiveness of the assessment process. Certainly, accurate assessment of performance is critical for effective performance management. Another important outcome of the process is the use of feedback to improve performance and develop employees. Even if the feedback generated is accurate, the process itself cannot be deemed successful if feedback is not accepted and applied to behavior. Thus, an often overlooked criterion for appraisal process success is appraisal reactions—namely perceptions of fairness and satisfaction. Research suggests that if employees believe that the process was fairly conducted, and they are satisfied with it, they are more likely to heed the feedback and use it to adjust or enhance behavior. The five-step process outlined below provides suggestions for a process that will generate positive reactions from staff.

Rather than a single event, chairs and other supervisors are encouraged to think of this as an ongoing process. This process best occurs when both parties are active and take responsibility in each step of the performance management cycle. Each step describes a specific event or set of behaviors that should occur; however, an assumption of this model is that performance feedback is shared by the parties throughout the process. Although the final step is a formal summary of performance over the year, feedback should be provided to employees continuously throughout the year.

The first step is to clearly establish the job responsibilities; this requires that both parties share information, ask questions, and seek clarity at the beginning of the performance cycle and throughout the year. In the second step, both parties need to calibrate and establish a common frame of reference for the behavioral expectations that underlie the job responsibilities. For instance, the department's fiscal officer might have budget reports as one job responsibility. It is the supervisor's responsibility to express behaviorally what it means to meet expectations for that duty. The behavioral expectation may include a statement of frequency of delivered reports (i.e., quarterly reports) and include a statement about the quality/accuracy of the reports (i.e., reports are generated with few if any mistakes). Developing criteria and standards that are clearly understood will allow individuals to more effectively self-regulate behavior to meet those goals.

The third step in the cycle is to monitor and collect performance indicators. Again, both parties are responsible for routinely assessing performance against the goals and cataloguing examples of success and/or failure to meet goals. This is especially important for staff positions where the outcomes of the work are not readily seen by the supervisor (e.g., number of IT issues addressed by an IT team). In these situations, we encourage supervisors to collect performance feedback or evidence from others that staff members may work with. For instance, your fiscal officer may work directly with a campus officer that may be able to provide meaningful feedback about the staff member's performance. The point here is that a fuller conversation about performance over the year can only happen if the supervisor has evidence of behavior across the year.

The fourth step is to evaluate performance prior to the interview. It is recommended that both the supervisor and the employee individually complete a performance assessment form. This encourages the employees to spend time thinking about their performance and preparing for the interview. It also provides the employee the opportunity to have some voice in the process. Research strongly supports the importance of voice for ensuring perceptions of procedural justice and fair treatment. Finally, if the supervisor sees the self-assessment before the interview, they can pre-identify areas of agreement or disagreement.

The final step is the interview, which often generates anxiety for both parties. However, if the steps above have been followed, and both parties have actively communicated throughout the year, the anxiety should be mitigated to a great degree. However, supervisors should consider these suggestions before the meeting:

- Both supervisors and staff should prepare for and formulate their goals for the meeting.
- The supervisor should ensure that there is ample, uninterrupted time for the meeting.
- Start with the self-assessment. Through active listening, the chair/supervisor may gain information that could adjust perceptions and create avenues for follow-up questions.
- Make sure that feedback focuses on specific examples and behaviors. Using generalities or focusing on personal characteristics is counterproductive and raises defensiveness.

- The supervisor should be prepared to offer developmental support for high-performing staff as well as appropriate support for those needing improvement.
- It is important that the supervisor maintain emotional equilibrium.

Staff in our academic departments are professionals, and treating them as such, including providing them with thorough, fair performance reviews along with help in improving or expanding skills, can boost morale and may enhance department productivity.

Reprinted from *Academic Leader,* December 2016

The Research Process and Its Relevance to the Culture of Assessment

Patrick J. Hughes, PhD

As higher education evolves, so too does the importance of assessing learning. New regulations, financial constraints, and accrediting agencies are stressing that colleges and universities should strengthen assessment organizationally. However, when assessment is discussed in large faculty forums, the concept often, strangely, becomes very foreign to them. Here is where understanding and employing the process of research can be very helpful in completing such tasks.

Historically, the process of research is associated with tenure, publications, and the doctoral process. Through the passage of time, research is now a balanced undertaking between gaining content knowledge and the process one goes through creating new knowledge. In breaking the traditional mold, it appears that having an understanding of the process of research may also help institutions in another area. This article examines the usefulness and paralleling of the research process and its application to institutional and academic assessments.

Every institution of higher education has a mission that all the institutional-level objectives should reflect. It does not stop there. Each program, as we know, has its own set of program-level objectives that should reflect the institutional-level objectives. Moreover, at the very bottom level are the course-level objectives that need to be met by students upon completing each course. Program chairs and directors are tasked with making sure every full-time, adjunct, and contracted instructor of that program is performing assessments of classes and linking them to the program objectives.

This task is easier said than done for two reasons. First, the number of adjuncts instructing in any one program could be so large as to cause a governance nightmare. Second, only recently has developing faculty on assessment become a more prevalent development option. Unlike K-12 teachers, who are often directly educated and certified in pedagogy and assessment, the large majority of college professors are not.

What then can institutions lean on to help this situation if professional development is not working or not an option? One consistent characteristic among collegiate faculty is they, at some point, have navigated the process of research. Those who were able to survive and thrive through that process should have learned something above the mere knowledge within their degree field. Each person did go through the process of creating knowledge. Is this not what we seek to obtain through assessing program objectives? The many parallels that the process of research holds with the assessment process became apparent after some reflection. Table 1 illustrates the comparison.

It is noteworthy that both processes are investigations at their very core. Here the assessment is investigating whether learning has occurred and to what extent. The process of research is investigating to create new knowledge or add support to an existing topic. Each process seeks to answer specific questions. The proper method must be employed to answer such questions. Finally, results in both processes need to be interpreted and conclusions made regarding the findings.

Ultimately, both the processes cycle back and start over again to provide a constant learning mechanism. It may be noted that the assessment completed for a course is searching for a definitive answer, while the dissertation seeks whatever outcome is achieved. While this has some validity, perhaps look at it in a manner to bring these two thoughts into close alignment. Assessment is completed in a course to see whether learning has occurred. Prior to doing the assessment, we only hypothesize that learning has occurred. This then becomes very similar to the hypothesizing that occurs during the process of research. The focus then becomes not so much about the outcome but about the process and why we are going through it. Assessment expert Linda Suskie (2009) states, "If faculty and staff find it hard to make the leap from articulating processes to articulating outcomes, encourage them to ask 'why?'" The question of why resonates in the dissertation process as well. I can remember my committee members telling me "You need to focus and answer the 'why.'"

It is important for curriculums to move away from simply memorizing numbers or regurgitating terms. Kelting-Gibson (2013), while discussing the work of David Perkins, echoes these similar sentiments. "It is important for students to develop understanding and not just memorize facts and figures." As our curricula continue to evolve, so too should our program objectives and the assessments that measure those in order to create deeper learning. The one constant we could rely on is reverting to the process of research to assist us with this evolving change. Doing this may ease the angst when program reviews and reaccreditation time roll around.

Process of Inquiry	Research	Assessment
Why	The overall purpose of the study and connection to the larger field	Overall goal (course description) students should obtain from the course and the connection to the program as a whole
What	The research questions designed to investigate the why	Course objectives of the course used to meet the overall goal
Who	Audience benefiting from the study	Students participating in the course
How	Methodologies (quantitative, qualitative, or mixed methods) used to answer the research questions (surveys, interviews, historical analysis)	Types of assignments or activities that will measure whether objectives are being met (i.e., research papers, exam questions, discussion boards, pretests and posttests, and also direct and indirect measures)
Conclusion	Use and analysis of results to support or refute the research goal and provide insight into future research	Use and analysis of results to support or refute that learning occurred and objectives have been met, as well as to indicate possible improvements to the program in future

Table 1: Process comparison

Reprinted from *Academic Leader,* December 2015

Using Formal Program Review for Continuous Improvement

Rob Kelly

Drexel University uses a Program Alignment and Review (PAR) process to help ensure relevance, quality, and measurable achievement of its academic programs. It's a formal review process that includes a self-study, external review, and action plan.

In an interview with *Academic Leader*, Janice Biros, senior vice provost for budget, planning, and administration, and Stephen DiPietro, associate vice provost for university assessment operations, discussed the process and outcomes of this effort, now in its third year.

Biros was an early advocate of a formal program review process. She felt there was a need to look at how the university was allocating its resources and supporting its priorities. Rather than focusing on resource allocation (although this would be an important component of the process), the provost decided on a more positive continuous quality improvement process.

From the start, Biros and DiPietro provided support rather than driving this initiative. A steering committee came up with a plan, timeline, guidelines, and tools. "It was all driven by the deans. They would identify which programs they wanted reviewed and when. They would identify the self-study groups and keep the process moving," Biros says. "I think it's unique in that it probably is a more formalized approach than many schools are taking. It has presidential and senior-level support, and I think it's beginning to take hold."

Self-study

PAR is a one-year process that begins with a self-study. A self-study committee of three to five faculty members selected by the dean and directed by the program coordinator or department chair conducts the self-study, which is based on the following data:

- **Program course catalog data**—required courses, electives, core major requirements
- **Student activity data**—10-year reports for enrollment, student credit-hour production, graduate rates, retention and persistence rates, GPA, and student learning assessment plan
- **Faculty profile**—10-year report of all employees by type, one-year faculty instructional workload report, 10-year report of external funding awards and applications, and CVs for each faculty member
- **Budget and finances**—10-year report of year-to-date expenses
- **Other resources**—list of library resources, report on facilities and space, the college strategic plan, the college organizational chart, the program strategic plan, the program organizational chart, experiential learning opportunities, and senior exit survey

This data is benchmarked against the college and the university to provide the self-study committees with some perspective on the data and how it compares to that of other programs.

The office of the provost supports the self-study committees, and a handbook (*www.drexel.edu/provost/par/assets/pdf/PARHandbook2014-2015.pdf*) provides detailed guidelines on the process.

The self-study report includes the following elements: an executive summary; program description; background and history; enrollment and student profile; faculty profile; curriculum and instruction; quality of program outcomes and learning assessment; research, scholarship, and creative activity; advising; finances; analysis of resources; facilities and space; technology; strategic alignment; and conclusion and action plan.

External review

To get a broader perspective on the program, the PAR process calls for an external review by up to three outside reviewers/scholars who conduct a site visit and produce a report that addresses many of the same questions addressed in the self-study.

Action plan

Based on the findings of the self-study and recommendations from the external review, the program creates an action plan that provides direction for the next seven years, which is when the next PAR takes place.

Results

Thus far, 23 programs have participated in the PAR process, and 13 are currently engaged in the process. The process has gotten faculty and academic leaders to consider their programs in a broader context. "I had a meeting with chemical engineering and one of the professors told me that he never really understood the curriculum until the PAR process. It provides an opportunity to see it from beginning to end," DiPietro says. "We're finding that PAR is facilitating discussions that have not occurred in the past."

PAR findings inform decisions, some of which can be implemented at the program level and some that require broader participation and resources.

"I think one of the things that's kind of interesting is that we ask [academic programs] to make recommendations for changes, and at the beginning everybody was saying, 'Where are the resources for all of this?' There is really not a budget for PAR. We're trying to integrate changes into other initiatives. For example, faculty hiring recommendations from PAR will be integrated into our overall university faculty hiring plan. And renovations and additional space requests are being integrated into our master planning and renovation process," Biros says.

A PAR task force on computing found very similar computing courses being offered across five colleges and schools. A group of faculty studied how the university taught computing and recommended creating a College of Computing and Informatics and bringing those courses together in one place. "It's a much more efficient and effective way to approach it," Biros says.

The PAR process does not drive decisions. PAR results inform decisions, and Biros and DiPietro are careful in the way they explain its intent and process. The goal is for the institution to make more informed decisions that drive academic quality. Thus far, changes have not resulted in major spending reductions "but, I believe, a more rational allocation of resources," Biros says.

The implementation of PAR comes at a time when the university is moving from traditional budgeting to responsibility-centered management (RCM), which gives deans more authority in managing their budgets. "The whole culture is changing," Biros says. "People are looking at information differently. People who didn't think about budgets before now are. And PAR is just another component of examining what we're doing. PAR is going to help deans as they manage their budgets. While RCM is not going down to the program level, clearly, when deans have to make decisions about their resources and they're going to budget, they'll have information from PAR to look at to prompt or support decisions they might make."

Reprinted from *Academic Leader,* March 2015

Preparing and Using Classroom Observations in Faculty Teaching Evaluations

Peggy Thelen, PhD

Evaluation of faculty teaching plays an important role in the success of the individual faculty member, the department, and, most importantly, student learning. And yet, many department leaders have had no formal training in observing and evaluating teaching. As the education world becomes increasingly evidence-driven, it is more crucial than ever to create appropriate and consistent faculty teaching observation models. It seems most prudent to use an evaluation process as a means to improve teaching, which, in turn, should improve learning. Teaching observation and evaluation should not be an excruciating process that a faculty member must try to "survive." It should be a beneficial, positive process that supports faculty teaching development.

The following is a model that (1) helps the evaluator and faculty member prepare for the observation, (2) provides the evaluator with a list of items to be observed, and (3) provides a look at what feedback and reflection are important after the observation. As always, the evaluator must keep in mind the importance of context-specific observation and evaluation. For example, an evaluator will be observing a faculty member teaching a biology lab differently than a faculty member giving a history lecture.

The three-step process is fairly intuitive, but a written document will aid in the consistency of the process across faculty evaluations.

Step 1: Pre-observation discussion with faculty member

The pre-observation discussion should center on what will be specifically observed, including what the faculty member wants the evaluator to observe and those foundational items that the department or institution says must be evaluated. This could include various goals or standards of teaching and learning. A mutually beneficial time for the evaluator to observe should be arranged. Surprise visits from an evaluator may not be in the best interest of either party. Planning to observe a faculty member only to have that person showing a long video or hosting an invited guest may be a waste of valuable time. There should also be mutual agreement as to the length of the observation as well as the number of observations, if there is no department or institution standard.

The faculty member and evaluator should agree on what materials the faculty member will provide ahead of time, including such things as the course syllabus, any assignments that may be discussed, a copy of lecture notes or a lesson plan, or any other materials that will be helpful in the observation and evaluation process.

Step 2: Classroom observations

There are a host of things that the evaluator will be noting during an observation. These include:

- Knowledge of the subject matter
- Effective presentation of the subject matter
- Organization of course materials (all materials needed are present; distribution of materials is planned)
- A structured approach to the presentation of the subject matter
- Clear explanations of course concepts and expectations; explained in different ways if necessary
- Appropriate pedagogy, including *active learning* experiences
- Tries to reach many learning styles
- Passionate when presenting the subject matter
- Student engagement throughout the class period

The evaluator will also want to note if the instructor uses any forms of assessment of student learning. Is there ongoing informal assessment such as questioning? Do the students have a chance to discuss concepts in small or large groups? Are there any in-class activities that solidify learning or can be used to test student learning? Also important is whether the assessments match the objectives of the lesson. Is there any remediation or reteaching if students do not understand the concepts or subject matter?

One of the most important aspects for an evaluator to note is the faculty member's relationships with students. Points of observation of positive relationships include:

- Mutual respect of the students by the faculty member and of the faculty member by the students
- Ethical behavior by the faculty member and students
- A classroom environment that is safe and open; students feel free to ask questions, voice opinions, answer questions, and engage in discussions
- Appropriate classroom management techniques; students respond positively
- The use of humor (not essential, but often important)

Step 3: Post-observation meeting

After the observation(s), it is essential that the evaluator and faculty member have a chance to debrief together in a timely and unrushed manner. To start the conversation, the evaluator may want to ask the faculty member his or her thoughts on the lesson. This gives the faculty member a chance to reflect on his or her teaching first and can give the evaluator insight into the confidence and best-practice beliefs of the faculty member. The evaluator can then give a more focused response. The evaluator should always start with positive feedback. Find something to confirm, even if it is to note how professionally the faculty member dressed or that the faculty member appeared to be very passionate about the subject matter. Starting off with criticism will immediately put the faculty member on the defensive—not a good communication technique.

It is just as important not to say anything you don't mean. Don't allude that something is terrific when it isn't. It is unfair and disrespectful (some may even say unethical) to lead a faculty member to believe that he or she is a pedagogical wonder when it isn't true. Remember to give feedback on the standards or "musts" observed as well as on the other agreed-upon items. Constructive feedback should be given so that the faculty member understands why the evaluator is giving this specific feedback and suggestions to improve. Feedback without suggestions feels like criticism.

Always save a little positivity for the end of the conversation. Again, a positive observation does not have to be award-worthy, just something that the faculty member can take away and feel good about.

There should be some time for questions and clarifications by both the evaluator and the faculty member. If necessary, a written plan for faculty member improvement may be created. This may include specific, realistic goals and how to reach these goals. There may be a timeline for the achievement of the goals included.

Faculty evaluations should be viewed as an opportunity to affirm those best-practice teaching skills that are present, as well as encourage and plan for the continuation of improvement of other skills. A department leader who appropriately supports and inspires has faculty who feel valued and appreciated.

Reprinted from *Academic Leader,* May 2015

Is It Worth Revisiting Faculty Evaluation?

N. Douglas Lees, PhD

Faculty evaluation is a very old subject that never seems to go away. New volumes on the subject continue to appear and articles are found with regularity in periodicals for university administrators. In addition, conferences for chairs usually have a number of sessions on this topic on the agenda. The books would not be published, the articles would neither be written nor accepted, and the conference sessions would not be held unless they were purchased, read, or heavily attended, respectively. Thus, there is a continuing appetite for information on this topic.

A recent national survey of department chairs (Cipriano, R. E. and Riccardi R. L., *The Department Chair*, 25(2), 3-4, 2014) identified evaluating faculty as the number one essential skill for chairs. At the same time, conducting annual faculty evaluations shows up high on the list of unpleasant chair tasks. One might conclude that the answer to the title question is "yes."

A new level of attention on issues concerned with faculty evaluation emerged about 15 to 20 years ago. A major factor in this new emphasis is the accountability movement in higher education, in which institutions have to demonstrate their value and effectiveness, and faculty must justify holding tenured positions by ensuring continued productivity and teaching success. This has culminated in many institutions requiring substantive post-tenure reviews of all faculty as a way of avoiding the threat of legislatures to eliminate tenure altogether.

In this case, "substantive" means a thorough review, one with the consequence of dismissal if unsatisfactory performance is not addressed within a defined period of time. To place this in an extreme context, imagine this change for an associate professor who is new to the chair position and who must evaluate, for the first time in two decades, a senior, full professor who has been performing poorly for years without consequence. This chair would almost certainly feel the need for advice.

A second factor impacting the faculty evaluation came into play with the elimination of mandatory retirement. While this is not always a negative (many of our senior colleagues still function at high levels), it can be a problem when some of these faculty are no longer competitive for funding, struggle with technology, or do not connect with today's students due to generational differences.

The frequency of faculty staying on has been exacerbated by economic factors and by the rapidly rising cost of health care. Faculty caught in these situations are often disappointed that they must stay when they had hoped to be elsewhere. Chairs facing reviews of this population are challenged on one hand to evaluate on the local standards of productivity, while on the other having the responsibility for helping these faculty through referrals to campus resources, modified assignments, special assistance, and personal wisdom.

The process, step by step

Assuming that there is an annual faculty evaluation process, where does the new chair begin in preparing for the process? This is an especially critical question if the chair is an external hire and is, thus, someone who has never been through the local process.

A recommended first step is the establishment (or review), with the collaboration of the faculty, of a set of measures and standards for performance in the areas of faculty responsibility (teaching research/scholarship, service, and others, in accord with institutional tradition). The list of items should have both quantitative and qualitative components (how many? how well?) and be as varied as is feasible.

Having multiple measures allows for individual faculty activities, strengths, and interests. Elements of the list can be aspirational in the sense that they are an attempt to develop new behaviors, and placing them on the list sends the message that they matter (or will) "count." Collaboratively defining the evidences to be used in the process of faculty evaluation is an important step because it brings clarity and a sense of ownership to the faculty.

Following from step one, the chair must collect data on the established measures. Much of this should come from the faculty member's written or electronic annual report. Additional information (e.g., surveys, evaluations done by peers and students, grant activity) may be provided by others.

Once the chair has all the information and has reviewed the previous year's evaluation with special emphasis on goals for achievement or, in some cases, for improvement, the next step is to schedule face-to-face meetings with each faculty member. The recommendation to meet with the faculty is based on the experience that much is revealed during the conversation.

The one-on-one meeting has importance beyond confirming and updating the data input. It provides the chair with the opportunity to give feedback to all. In some cases, it can be as simple as saying things like "your performance across all areas of responsibility has been stellar," or "you have met or exceeded all of your ambitious goals set last year." Earned accolades have a positive impact on future performance. The chair should be attentive to opportunities to provide formative feedback to help even high-performing faculty meet their goals. Adding a statement to the comments above, such as "I will provide resources for a visit from your new collaborator in order to facilitate the development of your joint proposal," might be an appropriate way to pledge support.

Some of the faculty, hopefully only a few, will be found to be in need of improvement. While this could be one of those difficult conversations, the chair should make the case based on the evidence and listen carefully to the response. In those cases where there is denial of responsibility, the chair must be firm in setting the expectation that improvement be made. To demonstrate support to effect the changes necessary and for the efforts of the faculty member, the chair should be prepared to offer or direct the faculty member to appropriate assistance.

In both the case of outstanding faculty performance and that of needed improvement, the chair should be prepared to offer support that will facilitate further growth or change the trajectory, respectively. This mandates that chairs become familiar with campus resources and what they have to offer (e.g., Center for Teaching Excellence, Research Office for grant writing) and that they develop a cadre of faculty who can serve as mentors/consultants or as connections to others across campus and perhaps beyond. In those cases where concrete resources are required (e.g., for travel, a student assistant, released time, an instrument), department budgets may be tapped or appeals made to the dean, with the latter prearranged where possible.

A final element of the meeting is to set goals for the coming year. This exercise serves the purposes of helping faculty structure their work, demonstrating chair interest in and commitment to success, and, in cases where performance is lagging, setting expectations for improvement. It also gives the chair a starting point for reviewing faculty accomplishments in the next review cycle.

Now it is time to author or revise the written review. This should follow from the conversation, with all evaluative remarks supported by evidence from the collected materials. This is another opportunity for praising excellence, pledging support, and setting the bar for improvement. Many colleges and universities use specific language to describe the level of faculty performance; the recommendation is that chairs use this language to avoid ambiguity. Revisions to correct errors of fact are acceptable, but chairs should take care to avoid negotiating language that diminishes the rightful impact of the evaluation. The final acts of the process are both parties signing off on the final document and submission by the chair.

What has been presented here is a skeletal structure with several recommendations for chairs who are new to or uncomfortable with conducting faculty evaluations. The final recommendation is that they review the literature on faculty career stages and on facilitating faculty career path changes for additional insights on maintaining faculty vitality.

Reprinted from *Academic Leader,* February 2016

Teacher and Peer Assessments: A Comparison

Maryellen Weimer, PhD

Interest in and use of peer assessment has grown in recent years. Teachers are using it for a variety of reasons. It's an activity that can be designed so that it engages students, and if it's well designed, it can also be an approach that encourages students to look at their own work more critically. On the research front, some studies of peer assessment have shown that it promotes critical thinking skills and increases motivation to learn. In addition, peer assessments are a part of many professional positions, which means they're a skill that should be developed in college.

But for teachers, there are several lingering questions. What kind of criteria are students using when they assess each other's work? Are those criteria like the ones their teachers are using? Given the importance of grades, can students be objective, or do they only provide positive feedback and high marks? To what extent do peer assessments agree with those offered by the teacher?

Falchikov and Goldfinch's (2000) meta-analysis of 48 studies of peer assessment published between 1959 and 1999 reported a moderately strong correction of .69 between teacher and peer assessments done by students. A large educational psychology team decided it was time to update that research, especially given a significant number of digital peer assessments are now being completed. They also wanted to learn more about the impact of certain factors on peer assessments.

This team analyzed 69 studies published since 1999. Unlike Falchikov and Goldfinch, they included studies done in K-12 grade levels, although there were a small number of them. They found the estimated average

Pearson correlation between peer and teacher ratings was also moderately strong at .63.

Most interesting in this recent research are findings about factors related to peer assessment. Here are some highlights:

- When the peer assessment is computer-assisted, the correlations drop to .50, but the researchers note a couple of issues. There is wide variation in the kind of computer involvement in peer assessment, and some studies provided no detail as to how computers were used. So, more research is needed. But the correlation is significantly higher if the peer assessments are paper based.
- As might be expected, the correlations were higher in graduate courses than in undergraduate courses.
- Group assessment correlations were significantly lower than individual assessments. The researchers hypothesize this is because assessment in groups involves interactions among group members and the dynamics within the group.
- Voluntary peer ratings showed more agreement with teacher ratings than when the peer assessments were compulsory.
- Interestingly, the correlations were also higher when the identity of the peer rater was known. Related research has documented that when the ratings are anonymous, the raters tended to be harsher. Also, when the rater identity is revealed, there may be a greater chance that the rater will take the task seriously, which means paying closer attention and thereby providing more accurate ratings.
- The correlations between teacher and student ratings were at .69 when students provided both a rating score and comments. Having to make comments forces reviewers to look carefully at the work and develop a rationale for their rating.
- When peer raters were involved in developing the assessment criteria, the correlations jumped to .86. The research team describes this finding as "striking": "Discussion, negotiation, and joint construction of assessment criteria is likely to give students a great sense of ownership and investment in their evaluations" (p. 256). It also makes the criteria easier to understand and apply.
- A big surprise was that training the peer raters was not a variable that resulted in significantly higher correlations between peer and teacher assessments. The researchers think that the variable quality of the training across the studies may have made its effect difficult to capture.

What is noteworthy about this meta-analysis is the attempt to identify factors that affect the accuracy of student judgments about the work of their peers. The analysis assumes that teacher assessments are the gold standard. Students should be making assessments similar to those of the teacher. It is useful to know those factors that help to close the gap between teacher and student assessments. The research team notes, "We included only theoretically meaningful predictors that could be reliably coded. As a result, the current meta-analysis explained only about one-third of the variation of the agreement between peer and teacher ratings" (p. 258). This means there must be other factors influencing the correlation. For example, could the correlations be affected by whether the ratings were formative, designed to help the recipient improve, or whether they were summative, as in counted as part or all of the grade?

This is relevant work with findings that should be considered in the decision to use peer assessments. As with so much of the research on instructional practices, the issue is less whether a particular approach is viable and more about the best ways to use it.

References:
Falchikov, N., and Goldfinch, J. (2000). Student peer assessment in higher education: A meta-analysis comparing peer and teacher marks. *Review of Educational Research, 70* (3), 287-3.
Hongli, L., Xiong, Y., Zang, X., Kornhaber, M., Lyu,Y., Chung, K., and Suen, H. (2016). Peer assessment in the digital age: A meta-analysis comparing peer and teacher ratings. *Assessment & Evaluation in Higher Education, 41* (2), 245–264.

Reprinted from *The Teaching Professor,* January 2017

Putting Assessment in Its Place

Kayla Waters, PhD, LP, and Zach Frank, PT, DPT, MS, CSCS, CEAS

What can you do with four minutes? You can close down the report and check the clock, update your to-do list, sort through your mail, or respond to a minor email query. There are lots of important tasks you can do in four minutes. And if you don't do them now, you'll just have to find another four minutes later. Of course, none of this matters if you have plenty of time and too little to do, but most institutions have finite resources and must be deliberate in how they use them. Program assessment presents a special challenge to resource allocation, requiring a similarly deliberate approach.

Importance of program assessment

Program assessment is a critical task in higher education. It is mandated by accrediting bodies and indispensable in the quest to provide high-quality programs that are well-received by students, communities, and other key stakeholders. Furthermore, from the finest of arts to the hardest of sciences, one mission of all academic programs is to promote critical evaluation of the products and processes of the field. To fail to apply a similar analysis to our own work would lack integrity.

Program assessment's place in academia

While program assessment is important, it is not and should not be mistaken for an essential function of academic institutions. While different institutions pursue different missions, none of us exist primarily for the purpose of assessing our own effectiveness. Assessment should be explicitly identified as subservient to our essential functions.

There are three reasons that assessment is a special case in resource allocation:

1. For any institution with finite resources, there is an inherent contradiction of purpose in program assessment. Every four minutes spent on assessment is four minutes not spent on the essential functions being assessed. While assessment should help us make our teaching better, too much assessment will make our teaching worse by diverting resources away from the very functions we are assessing.

2. The relative newness of the age of accountability in higher education creates urgency within a context of uncertainty over what will be considered acceptable by accrediting bodies. A natural response to the combination of pressure and uncertainty is to err on the side of over-performance, diverting too many resources away from essential functions in an effort to bolster assessment.

3. Though methodologies vary wildly, many academicians have great expertise in critical evaluation. Furthermore, in academia we find a high concentration of people who are constitutionally inclined to strive for the "top grade" on all tasks, regardless of relative priority.

Of course, assessment is important and worth investing in. Ideally, exactly the right resources in exactly the right quantity at exactly the right time will be assigned to each and every task. Because this level of precision is impossible and prohibitively costly to pursue, institutions must choose their errors by selecting which functions to over-support and which to minimally support. Because of its nonessential nature and inherent contradiction of purpose, assessment should fall into the second category.

Why lean?

Many academicians have virtually no training in resource allocation. Furthermore, academia sometimes lacks the direct feedback mechanisms more apparent in traditional businesses, especially at the department level where assessment plans are developed.

A few core principles from the Lean Six Sigma model can help departments keep assessment "in its place." Simply, "lean" means creating more value for customers while using fewer resources. This approach involves identifying all the tasks of the institution and analyzing each from the perspective of the customer. While academia serves many customers, we will focus here on students and their future employers.

Once customers have been identified, it is important to understand their voice by determining which institutional tasks are of value from their perspective. These value-added activities are defined as tasks for which the customer is willing to pay. However, some non-value steps are prerequisites for value-added tasks. Any unnecessary non-value-added tasks are considered waste. Once defined, the tasks can be prioritized. Value-added activities are supported and necessary, but non-value-added tasks are minimized, and waste is eliminated (Barry, Murcko and Brubaker, 2002).

Lean assessment planning

These core principles of Lean Six Sigma may be readily applied to program assessment in academia.

- Assessment planning should be student-centered and responsive to the needs of local employers and experts in the field. Students do not care if our assessment plans amaze our administrators and leave our accreditors in awe, and neither do the people who will hire them. Our customers want very good programs with very good reputations at a cost that makes sense. For institutions with finite resources, highly demanding assessment plans risk counterproductivity by diverting too many resources from essential (value-added) functions.

    For example, because many disciplines use student portfolios to assess department effectiveness, an array of sophisticated portfolio management software packages has joined the market. The lean approach asks us to consider whether this methodology would be student-centered.

- Assessment planning should be strategic. Every step of every process is evaluated for efficiency and waste. We should be on the lookout for practices that swallow up resources while yielding barely consequential (or negative) returns. For example, are the costs (time, energy, money) of purchasing, maintaining, learning, teaching, using, and evaluating the products produced with the portfolio software package justified by the expected gains to program outcomes?

- As a necessary but non-value-added task, assessment should be minimized. Minimizing doesn't mean that we treat assessment as unimportant. We should articulate a standard that meets the critical objectives of complying with accreditation requirements, improving program quality, and maintaining integrity, but we should accept that standard as "good enough" and purposefully go no further. Deliberately suppressing functioning to meet a good enough standard allows more resources to be directed toward essential functions. For example, even if the costs of portfolio management software seem justifiable, can the good enough standard be met through methods that are less costly?

- Assessment should be put in its place and kept there. The lean approach helps us remember that the more impressive an assessment plan in terms of the work and commitment it requires, the more likely that it is drawing valuable resources away from essential functions. Administrators should take the lead in designing processes for developing, implementing, sharing, and evaluating assessment plans that explicitly encourage departments to avoid misallocating excess resources away from essential functions. We should cultivate a knee-jerk wariness against being dazzled into over-resourcing nonessential tasks. We should evaluate assessment plans for value, strategy, and minimalism, and save the neat stuff for the classroom.

Assessment and beyond

The inherent contradiction of purpose in assessment makes it a low-threat vehicle for introducing lean efficiency principles to people who may have little training (and even less natural interest) in matters of efficient resource allocation. Once understood, the approach may be easily applied to a variety of domains of functioning. In financially-challenging times, when academic budgets are tight and faculty are called upon to model an ever-expanding wardrobe of hats, lean principles may allow departments to spontaneously prioritize their own processes to manage heavy workloads more effectively and stay student-centered. Remember, even four minutes can make a difference.

Reprinted from *Academic Leader,* July 2016

CHAPTER 3

•

Mentoring

Creating an Effective Mentoring Program

Kenneth L. Alford, PhD, and Tyler J. Griffin, PhD

I. Getting started

Recruiting and hiring new faculty is time intensive and expensive. Despite the difficulties, hiring decisions are clearly among the most important that academic administrators ever make. Success of college programs and universities is directly correlated with hiring the right people and then providing them with essential resources to succeed and excel in their work.

Teaching at the collegiate level is a wonderful yet complex career. We hire people and expect them to be organized, teach effectively, research thoroughly, write lucidly, publish often, serve as effective committee members, and maybe even serve as successful administrators. How many new hires on your campus arrive fully prepared and competent to fill that job description?

Far too often, a college's lofty expectations are not matched with appropriate training and resources for faculty members, especially during the more formative years. When a faculty member fails to meet expectations or falls short in the rank-advancement process, the time-consuming and costly process of recruitment and hiring starts over.

All new faculty hires have potential to become better teachers, researchers, writers, and administrators. Helping them reach their potential is the great challenge of creating and maintaining an effective mentoring program.

Since effective mentoring increases the likelihood that faculty members will be successful, designing and implementing a robust mentoring program is an essential part of a campus administrator's job rather than a distraction.

Even if little or no thought is given to a faculty mentoring program, a certain percentage of faculty members will seek out and obtain formative training from informal mentors on their own. Consider the risk of leaving this outcome to chance. More often than not, the disappointing result will simply confirm the aphorism: "If you fail to plan, you plan to fail." The reality is that "Mentoring sometimes has to be formalized, even mandated, or it simply will not occur" (Mullen 2012, 13).

College and department leaders can benefit from consciously considering several important questions when creating any organized mentoring program:

1. *Does my institution value mentoring?* Lip-service support is easy, but the easiest way to identify whether your institution truly values mentoring is to ask what specific resources will be devoted to supporting your program.

2. *What does mentoring currently look like at my institution?* What organized mentoring, if any, is currently being done with your faculty?

3. *How well is the status quo working?* Be honest. Analyze the degree to which your younger faculty members are progressing and meeting your department's expectations. Are there particular aspects of their work that consistently fall short or cause you frustration? What are your pain points with newer faculty?

4. *In a perfect world, what would my mentoring program look like?* Are there senior faculty members who could train younger faculty? How can I encourage and institutionalize mentoring interactions?

5. *What kind of ongoing financial and personnel resources would be required to support a mentoring program?* The key is ongoing resources. Mentoring is not a one-time project or one-day faculty meeting. Colleges and their faculties are seldom static. Hiring, firing, promotion, departures, retirement, and sometimes death can affect every faculty every year.

6. *How do I implement my envisioned mentoring program?* Nail it before you scale it. It is wise to organize a core group that can work out the kinks before adding new elements and complexity to your program.

Consider trying a pilot program

Managing a pilot mentoring program will require you to confront several difficult program-based decisions and questions, such as:

- *Funding.* Even though a pilot program will be less expensive and easier to fund than a full-scale program, it will still take financial commitment from school administrators. How will you convince key decision makers to provide those funds?

- *Scope.* Depending on the size and nature of your institution, you need to determine the pros and cons of implementing a mentoring pilot program at the department, college, or university-wide level.
- *Pairing choices.* How will you match mentored faculty members with their mentors? Will you create mentor matches from within the same discipline? The same department? The same college? The same campus?
- *Mentor guidelines.* Make the pilot program as representative of your future program as possible. Will you require mentors to be tenured faculty? Will you exempt administrators from serving as mentors? Success usually leads to success, so involve senior faculty who have demonstrated an ability to effectively handle their workloads and who have shown a propensity and capacity to train and lead effectively.
- *Mentee guidelines.* While you may wish to consider only full-time faculty for inclusion in the trial, consider how inviting one or more part-time or nontenured faculty members might increase the lessons learned for all participants.
- *Length.* How long do you need to determine what works and what doesn't? One year may be a reasonable starting point.
- *Evaluation.* How will you measure the effectiveness of your pilot program? Determine evaluation criteria before your pilot program begins.
- *Buy-in.* How will you get administrators, mentors, and mentees to really invest in your program? Each of these groups needs to clearly understand the benefits of participating. If you set clear standards and observable benchmarks, you will be more likely to expand beyond the pilot phase in the future.

II. Program Design Considerations

There are many ways to successfully organize an effective faculty mentoring program. Since one size doesn't fit all, campus leaders must determine the best use of available resources to meet the needs of new faculty members based on local circumstances, opportunities, and constraints.

When developing an effective mentoring program, there are several critical decisions you must make:

- *Formal mentoring, informal mentoring, or a combination.* Whether your institution uses a formal or informal mentoring program or some combination of the two depends on your situation. Formal mentoring programs can be administered with specified reporting requirements and accountability. Mentors and mentored faculty are formally assigned and publicly announced, with ongoing expectations for prescribed participation. The mentorship period could be as short as one semester or as long as it takes to help a mentee complete the tenure process. Informal programs tend to be more ad hoc and unstructured but can still be measured and incentivized.

- *One-to-one, many-to-one, many-to-many, or one-to-many.* Depending on your faculty structure, size, campus resources, and needs, you will need to determine what combination of mentor resources will best meet the needs of your newer faculty members. For some colleges, the simplest and most effective program will consist of pairing up mentors and mentees one-to-one. For larger faculties, you might find greater success in assigning mentor specialists who each work with new faculty members on one particular aspect of their training. Other faculties will find success with a one-to-many model where one mentor works with all new faculty members for a given amount of time.

- *Single mentor vs. team approach.* Finding "the perfect mentor" is unlikely. New faculty member A needs support and tutelage to improve both her teaching and scholarship. Senior faculty member X is an outstanding teacher, but is only a mediocre researcher and author. Senior faculty member Y is just the opposite. Under this scenario, faculty member A is far more likely to succeed with your department expectations if you assign X as her teaching mentor and Y as her research and writing mentor.

- *Mandatory vs. opt-in.* Will you make participation in your mentoring program mandatory—for both new faculty hires as well as potential senior faculty mentors? Or will you allow faculty members to opt in and out? While few faculty members will voluntarily seek more work, a mandatory program will generally serve your organization best in the long run.

- *Incentivized vs. non-incentivized.* Hoping that a non-incentivized program will be beneficial and receive the sustained wholehearted commitment of both mentors and mentees alike is betting against human nature. Providing incentive pay is certainly not the only option available. Student teaching and research assistance, lightened teaching or publication requirements, a guaranteed parking space, release from other department committee assignments, and many other alternatives can be creative ways to provide incentivized participation.

- *Entire faculty participation vs. selective participation.* Regardless of how the mentoring workload is shared among your senior faculty members, it will still result in more work for the faculty members involved. You and your faculty should have an open discussion regarding the benefits, costs, and responsibilities involved in supporting a meaningful mentoring program.

Several additional decisions will also need to be made before you formally begin your mentoring program, such as:

- Will your mentoring program be organized and administered at the university, college, or department level?
- Who will administer your mentoring program? Are there advantages to having separate administrators at each organizational level?
- What reporting responsibilities will your administrator, mentors, and mentees have?
- What goals do you have for new faculty who successfully complete your mentoring program?
- What part, if any, should active participation in your mentoring program have when making decisions regarding tenure or rank advancement?
- How will you measure your mentoring program's success or failure?
- How often should mentors and mentees meet? Monthly during the first semester can be a good starting point.
- What resources can your administrator prepare and provide to the mentors and mentees within your program? Successful mentoring experiences seldom just happen. Don't make mentors reinvent the wheel. Provide them with pertinent information that they can then contextualize for their mentees without requiring them to be the expert on everything (e.g. benefits, campus policies, legal questions, etc.).
- What program-wide activities will your administrator provide for mentoring program participants? Each semester, for example, you may wish to gather all mentors and mentees for a luncheon with an appropriate guest speaker.
- How long will mentor assignments last? One year? Two years? Through tenure application?

The more accurately you can envision your program in advance, the greater will be your success. Look for the sweet spot between organization and flexibility.

III. Steps to Building an Effective Program

Most administrators can easily generate a list of reasons why they need an effective faculty mentoring program. Many can also describe the desired outcomes of mentoring efforts. The struggle begins when they are confronted with questions regarding how to develop such a program and obtain buy-in from stakeholders at every level. Here are a few suggestions:

Step One: Analyze the cost/benefit of mentoring efforts. This begins with knowing how much time, energy, resources, and money are being spent on recruiting and hiring new faculty members. It also involves knowing the outcomes from past tenure processes. How much did each failed tenure candidate cost the department? Also, consider the costs and lost benefits to the department when some candidates gain tenure but fall short of excelling in their work. Once administrators clearly quantify and qualify these factors, they can proceed with more clarity and efficiency to achieve the desired mentoring program outcomes.

Step Two: Understand what leads to failure and what contributes to success. Begin by identifying the major challenges that consistently impede your faculty in the tenure process. What are their most predictable "pain points" when striving to meet research, teaching, or citizenship expectations? Which expectations are they consistently meeting or exceeding? What patterns emerge when contrasting the successes and struggles? Based on the outcomes of this analysis, an administrator can recognize which aspects to target through mentoring efforts.

Step Three: Assemble the right team to design and develop an effective mentoring program. At first, this step may seem like a no-brainer, but it is too often bypassed during program creation. Begin by identifying the "natural mentors" among your veteran faculty members, and seek their help in designing an effective mentoring program and a successful mentoring environment. These are usually the teachers newer faculty members inherently respect and approach for advice and direction. Provide the team members with the resources they need to succeed. When they fully understand the needs and potential benefits, have a shared vision for what is expected, and are given appropriate compensation for their time and effort, they are more likely to fully invest and give meaningful input. Guide them through the process to design a program that will best meet faculty needs. The more this small team is involved in program decisions, the more likely they are to feel shared responsibility for helping it succeed. They will also be more likely to help junior faculty develop to the point where they can be effective mentors for the next generation of instructors and scholars.

Step Four: Share your newly created mentoring program plan with higher administration and seek their buy-in. Explain the costs along with the numerous benefits of supporting such a program. Your senior leadership team will be more likely to give their support if they see a well-designed plan with measurable outcomes. They will look for a return on their investment of limited campus resources. You cannot proceed until you lock in program funding. Ideally, initial funding should be for a one-year pilot program. Administrator confidence will increase if your new program includes clear benchmarks with objective evaluation criteria to measure its effectiveness.

Step Five: Seek buy-in from department chairs. They know the needs of their department, the teaching workloads, and the strengths and weaknesses of their faculty members. Chairs are in a good position to give recommendations regarding which mentors should be the "best fit" for recently hired faculty. Chairs can also help identify possible resistance or concerns among participants.

Step Six: Actively work to obtain buy-in from your faculty—potential mentors and junior faculty alike. This could include appropriate incentives such as salary bonuses, cash awards, research funds, course reductions, scheduling flexibility, and parking privileges. Mentored faculty could also be offered appropriate incentives to encourage deeper engagement with your program. Getting participants fully "on board" will require more than just incentives, though. You may find it beneficial, for example, to dedicate time during department meetings to recruiting and educating your faculty about this effort.

Step Seven: Get started! Allow your design team and mentors flexibility to implement the program. Create a culture of effective feedback and teamwork so everyone can benefit from individual successes. Don't expect your mentors to be experts on everything. Even veteran professors can benefit from mentoring regarding how to be a more effective mentor. Keep a written record of lessons learned throughout your pilot program. Recognize that this will be an iterative learning process.

IV. Mentorship Dos and Don'ts

Faculty mentoring programs are only as good as the mentors who work with junior faculty. Unfortunately, few senior faculty members ever receive formal training regarding how to be an effective mentor. They may be excellent instructors and researchers in their subject areas. They may also be experts on university and department cultures and policies. But most will likely need direction and training to learn how to transmit their proficiencies to the next generation of faculty members.

The purpose of this article is to share suggestions to assist mentors—Dos and Don'ts—that have proven successful in a variety of faculty settings. Here are a few suggestions for mentors to consider:

Getting started

- **Don't** assume that you understand what your mentee hopes to gain from your mentoring. **Do** discuss expectations and define responsibilities for both of you.
- **Don't** talk too much. **Do** ask questions, listen, and try to understand how you can best help.
- **Don't** be too formal with your mentee. **Do** drop in on your mentee's (classrooms or office) when appropriate to show support and see how he/she is progressing.
- **Don't** be overpowering. **Do** establish a relationship of trust early.
- **Don't** make "You're doing great!" or "Don't change a thing!" comments unless you *really* mean them. **Do** give *specific* feedback, including constructive criticism when appropriate.
- **Don't** put your focus solely on what your mentee has done previously. **Do** focus on the kind of teacher and researcher your mentee has the capacity to become.
- **Don't** wait for mentoring interactions to happen. **Do** set regular mentoring meetings based on need (perhaps weekly, twice monthly, or monthly).

It's about them—not you

- **Don't** overwhelm your mentee with all that you have accomplished in your career. **Do** share vitas and discuss the mentee's goals and aspirations.
- **Don't** try to clone yourself. **Do** help your mentee develop his/her own talents, abilities, and experience.
- **Don't** smother or ignore your mentee. **Do** find the right balance that works for both of you, knowing this balance will naturally adapt over time.
- **Don't** do everything for your mentee; you are only a guide. **Do** help your mentee grow incrementally through the four stages of

development: (a) show, (b) help, (c) watch, and then (d) let.

- **Don't** pretend to know everything and make up answers to try to impress your mentee. **Do** model for your mentee how to really solve problems in your field and find answers to questions.
- **Don't** think you will do all the teaching and your mentee will do all the learning. **Do** establish a respectful relationship where you learn and grow from working with your mentee, and let him/her know when you learn something new from him/her.
- **Don't** try to be a "one-stop shop"—answering all of your mentee's questions. **Do** recognize that there are many times when referring your mentee to others will be more beneficial for him/her than re-solving a question or problem yourself.
- **Don't** overestimate or overstate your strengths. **Do** identify your strengths and weaknesses as a mentor and communicate them to your mentee.

Teach how things work

- **Don't** assume that your mentee understands "how things *really* work" in your department, college, and institution. **Do** have several discussions about "the basics":
  - What are department expectations regarding teaching, scholarship, and citizenship?
  - Are funds available to hire student teaching assistants and/or research assistants?
  - What are departmental expectations for office hours and meeting with students?
  - Are there department guidelines and expectations regarding grading?
  - Is there an institutional student evaluation system? If so, how does it work?
  - What faculty services are provided by your institution?
  - What teaching and research support is available for new faculty members?
  - What are the expectations, deadlines, and requirements regarding tenure?
  - What learning management system options are available?
  - What resources are available to help students with university accessibility exceptions (physical, emotional, or mental disabilities)?
  - What kind of information technology support is available?
  - How is pay determined in the department? What factors contribute to raises and merit pay?

- **Don't** assume your mentee understands how tenure works at your institution. **Do** guide your mentee through the tenure process.
- **Don't** involve your mentee with departmental infighting or old struggles. **Do** take time to share appropriate department culture with your mentee.

Mentors should not be expected to know all of the answers to these questions. One of the most supportive actions academic leaders can take is to let mentors know that your door is always open to support them in their mentoring efforts.

V. Mentee Dos and Don'ts

The ultimate test of a mentoring program is this: Did you provide the necessary resources and training to help new faculty members reach their potential?

You can have a perfectly organized, well-funded program with expert mentors, but without active and diligent engagement from your new faculty, your mentoring program will not succeed. This article contains tips and suggestions for new faculty members to help them benefit the most from mentoring efforts. Here are a few recommendations:

Getting started
- **Don't** wait for your mentor. **Do** take the initiative to establish a meaningful relationship with him/her.
- **Don't** overestimate your knowledge and abilities. **Do** seek your mentor's advice and assistance.
- **Don't** try to do everything at once. **Do** set personal goals and ask your mentor to review them to ensure that you will have no surprises working through the tenure process.
- **Don't** be resentful when advice is given to you. **Do** genuinely listen and apply the principles you learn.
- **Don't** have an "I must work 24/7" mentality. **Do** invite your mentor to help you find an appropriate balance between work and other important aspects of your life.

It *is* about you, but . . .
- **Don't** be overconfident or arrogant with your mentor, or he or she will stop giving you counsel and feedback, causing you to lose an advocate. **Do** recognize that you are a junior faculty member—be teachable and open to feedback and assistance.

- **Don't** see your formal mentor as your one and only source of help. **Do** establish many helpful informal mentoring relationships.
- **Don't** blindly do everything your mentor tells you. **Do** ask clarifying questions to better understand the underlying reasons for the direction and counsel so your work will be more purposeful and meaningful.
- **Don't** rely too heavily on your mentor. **Do** demonstrate your intelligence and initiative by producing excellent work without too much direction.
- **Don't** work in isolation from your mentor. **Do** encourage your mentor to help you be accountable for deadlines and expectations you set for yourself.

Learn how things work

- **Don't** be shy about asking your mentor questions. **Do** clarify workflow issues with your mentor (e.g., official travel authorization and funding, library policies, annual funding cycles, the hiring of teaching and research assistants, testing center policies, committee assignments, required meetings, inservice training, faculty support facilities, building maintenance, office supplies, computer support, parking, textbook orders).
- **Don't** assume that you understand "how things *really* work" in your department, college, and institution. **Do** ask questions such as the following:
  - What are the requirements in our department for teaching, scholarship, and citizenship?
  - How are each of these areas weighted and evaluated in the tenure process?
  - How important is peer-reviewed research in our department?
  - What publication venues are encouraged? Are any publication options discouraged?
  - How do various forms of publications compare with each other in the tenure process (e.g., books, chapters in edited publications, journal articles, and conference papers/presentations)?
  - What are the pros/cons of teaching the same courses repeatedly versus teaching a broad range of classes?
  - What is the required teaching load? What is a reasonable amount of time to spend on course preparation?
  - What are the expectations for selecting course content and textbooks?

- What learning management system (LMS) do we use? Where can I receive training on how to use it?
- How is outside professional service viewed (e.g., community outreach, review boards, journal editing, and conference committees)?
- What resources are available for helping students with physical, emotional, or mental disabilities?
- What resources are available for ongoing teacher development?
- What resources exist to answer questions about syllabi, exams, grading, office hours, technology use, library resources, interdisciplinary collaboration, writing workshops, and the like?
- What should be included in a teaching portfolio? What are some good and bad examples of past dossiers?
- What legal issues do we face, and what are the campus policies (e.g., risky student behavior, harassment, cheating and plagiarism, copyright and fair use, privacy, discrimination, Americans with Disabilities Act, and intellectual property)?
- What should I include or avoid in my vitae?
- **Don't** repeat past failures. **Do** find out from your mentor what other new faculty members have done that led to success or struggles in their work.

New faculty should be careful to avoid two extremes—being either too demanding of one's mentor's time or paying too little attention to him or her. One of the best ways to establish a meaningful mentoring relationship is for new faculty members to be genuinely responsive to and appreciative of support offered by their mentors.

VI. Mentoring Program Guidelines and Tips

At the beginning stages of a successful mentoring program, you must provide appropriate development and clear expectations for your mentors. Your program's success will largely depend on how well you mentor your mentors. Don't expect them to be expert mentors just because they may be excellent researchers or teachers.

You may wish to use a repeatable four-step pattern to foster self-reliance in your mentors:

1. Don't simply tell them what to do; *show them* what is expected.
2. Give feedback and guidance as needed to *help them* as they practice new skills.

3. Give them sufficient time and resources to work on new skills. Re-assure them that you are available, as needed, to *watch them* to see where additional support or redevelopment may be needed.
4. Give them the freedom they need to perform the tasks without your direct involvement, and *let them* put their own flair on it.

Help your mentors look for ways to use this same general pattern with their mentees. The further this process develops, the less involved trainers should become. As mentees assume more ownership and responsibility, their capacity to solve problems and resolve concerns should increase.

The following additional principles and practices can help program administrators work effectively with mentors and mentees:

- Don't try to demonstrate, guide, observe, and facilitate in a single development session. This is not a one-time event. It is a process that requires both time and patience.
- Carefully match mentors and mentees, and then monitor the working relationships that develop. What may have seemed like a perfect pairing at the outset might result in personality clashes, in-compatible teaching or research styles, or scheduling conflicts that may require administrative intervention.
- It can be an exercise in frustration if you require mentors to be-come experts in all aspects of new faculty development. Instead, identify issues (e.g., legal policies, human resource benefits, campus teaching and research resources, citizenship requirements, Amer-icans with Disabilities Act requirements, emergency procedures) that are generally applicable to all mentees and discuss them as a group. Rely on campus experts to present development on these topics. Doing so will allow your mentors to focus most of their ef-forts on improving the scholarship, teaching, and citizenship skills of their mentees.
- Set reasonable time commitments for program participants to avoid surprises and frustration. Otherwise, mentees may demand too much of their mentor's time or participate too little in their own development. It is important to establish realistic expectations early in the process regarding how long it should take (in months or years) to accomplish major mentoring program goals and mea-surable outcomes.
- Clearly establish your mentoring program objectives and commu-nicate them to all participants in multiple ways and on multiple occasions. Identify the key indicators for success with each

outcome. Also determine how those indicators will be measured and quantified.

- As with most things, don't assume that one size fits all. Nobody likes feeling victimized by unnecessary mandates or busywork. Give each mentor/mentee pair the freedom and flexibility to decide for themselves how to best accomplish program goals in a way that fits their unique situation. Wherever possible, provide program participants with choices and adequate resources to facilitate their success within the broad parameters you have set.

- Be careful to select only the most vital aspects of your program as key indicators for measurement and analysis. Recognize that whatever you emphasize and measure is also likely to become a focus of your mentors and mentees. Be certain that these "program measurables" are within the participants' control.

- Set appropriate intervals (perhaps monthly, quarterly, biannually, or annually) to collect and attempt to interpret formative research data on your key indicators. This review will allow you to discover potential negative aspects and unintended consequences of your program and make appropriate adjustments before behaviors become entrenched and threaten future success or funding. This also prepares the way for more predictability when administering summative evaluation on your program.

- Continue to look for meaningful and constructive ways to incentivize excellence within your mentoring program. Positive feedback, formative advice, and little perks along the way can help to ensure that your mentors and mentees stay focused on your program's objectives, rather than putting forth a flurry of activity shortly before announced deadlines.

Successful mentoring programs require clarity of focus, clear vision and expectations, open communication, frequent monitoring, appropriate adaptability, and ongoing development for the mentors. All participants, including supervisors and program administrators, must remain vigilant and active to ensure success.

VII. Developing a Culture of Mentoring Excellence

The old adage, "Give a man a fish, feed him for a day—teach a man to fish, feed him for a lifetime," helps only one person. In the context of faculty development, we suggest adding a third couplet: "Teach someone to teach others how to fish—feed a village for generations!" This addition describes a continually developing culture in which mentoring and training are fostered and intentionally infused into the experiences of junior faculty members.

There are several practical things administrators can do to help instill such a spirit of continual growth and mentoring within their faculty. Begin by focusing mentoring efforts on what type of scholars and educators faculty members are *becoming*. This becomes easier when you make an effort to consider more than just what faculty members already *know* or what they can already *do*.

Most institutions of higher education emphasize three areas when training and evaluating faculty members: scholarship, teaching, and citizenship. Traditionally, the first two dominate hiring and advancement decisions. In many settings, the reduced emphasis on citizenship may lead some faculty members to minimize or overlook mentoring duties and expectations. Insufficient mentoring today can contribute to faculty with inadequate teaching or research skills tomorrow.

Administrators who appropriately emphasize and incentivize citizenship endeavors are more likely to have faculties who spend appropriate time and effort fostering a culture of mentoring excellence. Such a culture requires clear and open communication between administrators, mentors, and mentees. Don't leave program outcomes to chance or random influences. Success in your mentoring program should be based on the purposeful efforts of everyone involved. Focus people's attention and energy on solvable problems. Help them set goals that are specific, measurable, rigorous, and attainable.

Mentoring excellence also requires the establishment of reasonable expectations together with objective benchmarks so faculty members don't feel as though they are aiming at a moving target. Mentoring objectives are best established and improved through collaboration and formative feedback from faculty members at all levels of your mentoring program. Clearly communicate expectations and subsequent modifications to everyone to minimize frustration, increase focus, and make success more likely.

Encourage mentees to pay close attention to all aspects of their mentoring experience. They will usually focus most of their attention on *what* they are being taught, but greater growth can come if mentees also pay attention to *how* they are being mentored—keeping track of what they liked as well as what they did not like, what worked and what efforts were less effective. When they anticipate their future roles as trainers and mentors, they will be more likely to internalize the *process*, not just the *products* of the mentoring they are experiencing. Generally, the most engaged learners become the most effective teachers and trainers.

Finally, be patient. Recognize that organizational cultures generally change slowly. When growing farm crops (and junior faculty members), flash floods are not nearly as effective at promoting lasting growth as trickle irrigation. Rather than chasing quick fixes and flashy results, take the long view. Seek to build a culture of mentoring excellence. Doing so can lead to increased trust within your campus community, especially between faculty and the administration. As future hires develop within your mentoring culture, they can build on the successes and lessons of the mentors who preceded them.

Effective mentoring programs are difficult to create and to maintain. They require many resources and great effort expended over long periods of time. The costs may seem daunting, but the alternative to not investing in such programs will be costlier and more time-intensive problems in the future. New faculty members are not a burden or a problem; they are the embodiment of your future solutions and success.

Get personally involved with mentoring. Invest appropriate time and effort to create a culture of mentoring excellence. If you train and encourage your mentors and junior faculty to build meaningful relationships with each other, many students and other faculty members will benefit as well.

Reference
Mullen, Carol A. 2012. "Mentoring: An Overview." In *SAGE Handbook of Mentoring and Coaching in Education*, edited by Sarah Judith Fletcher and Carol. A. Mullen, 13. London: SAGE Publications.

Reprinted from *Academic Leader,* 2017

Helping Faculty Develop a Scholarship Agenda

James O. Hammons, PhD

A major role of every academic leader is to help faculty do well. For those of us who work in institutions where becoming a productive scholar is an absolute prerequisite to earning tenure, "doing well" implies developing a scholarship agenda, and "working" a plan.

Ensuring that new faculty get off to a good start is a very important component of any successful plan. All too often we spend limited travel funds and go to extraordinary efforts to recruit promising candidates only to see them leave our institution because they realize they are not on track to earn tenure. Some, realizing they will not do well, leave as they approach their three-year review. Others stay until they fail their sixth-year "up or out" review. Both cases represent a lose-lose situation.

The individual (and their significant others) lose as they are uprooted and have to find another position—a task made more difficult by the circumstances of their departure. Institutions lose in several ways. Obviously, they must reapply to fill the position, make do while the position is vacant, and then conduct another time-consuming and expensive search. Not so obvious are several other consequences which, while even more costly, are often not recognized. For example, if the new faculty member was given a reduced load or increased travel funds, what effect did this have on departmental colleagues?

After an unsuccessful third-year review and being "put on notice," faculty members in that situation will choose one of two options, both of which represent a loss to the department. One option is to focus all their efforts on scholarship. As a consequence, teaching receives minimal attention; curriculum and instructional development suffer; and advising students and departmental service become a low priority. Other department faculty fill in the gap or the work doesn't get done. In addition, the uncertainty about their continuation affects both short-term and long-term planning of the department and, in some instances, this uncertainty can affect the work environment of the department.

Can this "lose-lose" situation be avoided—and, if so, how? The solution is not rocket science. One suggestion is to help the new faculty members succeed by asking them to set goals and develop a plan for achieving them;

meet with them to review their plan, then periodically review progress, offering help and advice as needed.

One way to help them focus—and help you better assist them—is to have them complete something like the following. Ideally, it should be done during their first three months.

Scholarship Agenda

Name: _____

Date of Initial Appointment: _____

1. **Purpose:** The purpose of this document is to assist both untenured and tenured professors in developing and pursuing a scholarship agenda and a plan for achieving it. By following this process, reviews of progress will be positive experiences.
2. **Definition of Scholarship:** In keeping with a growing national trend and in view of our mission as a land grant university (or our mission as a predominately teaching-oriented institution—tailor this to your institution), we have chosen to use the term "scholarship" as the umbrella term to encompass and encourage a broader range of activities than those included under the much narrower terms "research and publications."

   Scholarship is an inclusive construct that includes the many ways in which faculty draw upon their expertise in performing teaching, research, and service functions that directly relate to their specialized fields of knowledge or expertise. It can include all faculty work meeting the following criteria: (a) it requires a high level of discipline-related expertise; (b) it is public in the sense that it can be replicated or elaborated; (c) it can be documented; (d) it can be peer-reviewed; and (e) it has impact on/ or significance (for) external or internal communities directly affected by the effort or the discipline itself (Robert Diamond).
3. Please identify the major professional/academic organizations in your professional field of specialization, indicating whether you are currently a member of each, the extent of your current involvement, and your desired involvement in the future (attending meetings, serving on boards, acting as a program chair, presenting, etc.).

List Organization and Requested Information (Add more pages as needed.)

4. Please identify the leading national journals in your field of professional specialization, the ones which you read and your intended involvement in the future (serving on editorial board, publishing articles, etc.)

List Title(s) and Required Information (Add more pages as needed.)

5. Explain your major research agendas (topics) and for each topic you listed, please describe briefly any scholarly work already in progress and identify your co-workers (identifying each as student or faculty member). (Add more pages as needed.)

6. State what you hope or expect to have achieved in terms of pursuing your research agenda during the next 12 months, e.g., planned papers and presentations, and articles you hope to submit. Please be as specific as possible. List the organizations where you hope to present, journals in which you hope to publish, etc. (Note: This is a tentative projection on your part, not a contractual obligation or promise!) (Add more pages as needed.)

7. Given existing staffing and budgetary constraints, what could be done to facilitate your accomplishing the activities set forth in this document? (Add more pages as needed.)

Faculty Member_____ Date _____

Comments by Department Head (or Dean)

Department Head (or Dean) _____ Date_____

1 copy – faculty member's folder
1 copy – faculty member

Author's note:

While the major focus of this article is on helping untenured faculty develop and achieve a scholarship agenda, it can also be quite helpful in working with tenured faculty.

Please tailor as needed to fit your needs. I ask only two things. One, that you let me know if you use it. Two, that you notify me of its value to you—did it help?

Reprinted from *Academic Leader,* April 2016

Using Academic Retreats to Enhance Academic Affairs Performance

Henry W. Smorynski, PhD

Every academic leader invests time in strategic planning groups, presidential cabinets, councils of department chairs, dean's council meetings, and similar regularly scheduled meetings. Academic leaders occasionally leave the campus for meetings of professional societies or to participate with other academic leaders in retreats. What few institutional leaders do is develop a meaningful retreat on campus or at a location close to campus for a day or day-and-a-half for their academic team, including deans/assistant deans,
service units (registrar, counseling, support services), institutional research, budget officer, etc.), head librarian, and the secretaries servicing major officers.

Frequently, deans of academic affairs and vice presidents meet only with their individual direct reports, either on set schedules or for crisis consultations. This means that inter-unit collaborations are often not explored or fully developed, leadership messages are not understood in the same way by all team members, and faculty do not experience seamless relationships across academic affairs. These limitations generally lead to less successful execution of the academic mission and partial confusion and miscommunication about key academic directions.

What kinds of factors lead to the limited use of academic retreats to maximize academic affairs performance in service of the mission, faculty, students, and other administrative units of the institution? Probably one of the most important factors is that many service unit leaders are needed to problem solve and serve their units every day during regular school hours.

Another is that non-faculty units are often perceived to be of secondary value in academic affairs plans and successes. Further, some unit leaders feel uncomfortable working with peers they generally don't work with, and secretaries and administrative assistants generally do not see themselves as having much to offer in retreats. Finally, in most academic affairs departments there is a hectic atmosphere that causes many to see taking time out for retreats as time taken away from more vital activities and/or increasing their workload when they return from the retreats.

One generally has to communicate clearly the value of academic retreats to get buy-in and full and positive involvement from the entire academic team. It is vital that chief academic officers communicate the value they believe will be achieved by having an annual academic retreat. One of the most important values of a retreat is the support for consistency of message within academic affairs regarding standards and procedures and institutional direction, plans, and vision. A second value of academic retreats is the creation of a better understanding of the limits of the work environments and daily stresses encountered by each subunit. This understanding will inevitably lead to better sharing, more timely requests for assistance, and better acceptance of time requirements for meeting each other's needs. A third value is the full development of a team attitude among the members by their respecting each other's expertise and working for the success of each other's units. A fourth value is communicating with one another strategies that are working or not working in serving faculty, student, parent, and non-academic units' needs. A fifth and critical value is the opportunity to share information about the future challenges units will be facing due to knowledge from environmental scanning and peer professional meetings that will inevitably affect other units in academic affairs. Finally, retreats are a time for individual development of communications skills, empathy, professional self-confidence, and personal appreciation of the work of each member to ensure the success of the university's academic affairs.

The bottom line is that academic affairs retreats are an important time for interpersonal development in the hectic, challenging, and often isolating environments that can be experienced by most academic affairs staff members.

How can one develop a successful academic affairs retreat? The first issue to be resolved is to find a time that works for all parties. There is a rhythm to the academic calendar, and few dates can work for everyone. Generally, the best times are shortly before the spring or fall semesters begin or during student breaks. Once a common time is found, the next issue is to provide skeleton services in units either through other people in the units or, if the units are too small, through reduced hours set at the beginning and end of the work day; for example, the registrar's unit might be open from 8 to 9 am and then again from 4 to 5 pm only. It is critical that faculty, nonacademic staff, and students be informed about the retreat several weeks in advance with constant reminders through emails, posting signs on office doors, and other mechanisms common to the campus.

After one has established the day (or days) for the retreat and communicated them to the campus, the critical work of a successful retreat is achieved by carefully planning the day; it should be relaxed and informal. Food and snacks should be a part of the day, including a shared communal lunch. Sessions should break into 30- to 45-minute units with morning and afternoon breaks. Topics should be a mixture of substantive academic affairs issues and time should be set aside for team and personal development activities suited to the wide variety of participants.

What would be typical topics or activities to build into a retreat, eliminating some from a one-day retreat and adding others if the retreat is one-and-a-half days? Academic affairs vision, direction, and goals should always be included with time for questioning and clarification led by the chief academic officer. One unit of academic affairs should be highlighted, led by the unit's leader, to provide an in-depth understanding of that unit for better collaboration and for the unit leader's professional development. A key element of any retreat is sharing environmental scanning trends across all units that are likely to affect academic affairs in the future. At least for some years, one should bring in an outside person from another unit of the institution or an expert on some topic of relevance to academic affairs success such as changing students' attitudes or behaviors, handling difficult customers, or communicating with parents. In most years, a self-assessment/development session should occur with teams of individuals who don't usually work with each other. The session should cover such topics as conflict management, time management, communications styles, and reading body language. During lunch, a short praise session should be led by the chief academic officer to highlight exceptional performances. Finally, the retreat should end with a practical assessment of what worked and didn't work as part of the chief academic officer's summary of what was achieved. That should be followed by a thank you to everyone for participating.

Reprinted from *Academic Leader,* June 2012

Speed Mentoring

Kami Barrett and Jeffrey L. Buller, PhD

Mentoring is a common yet powerful way for people to learn a variety of personal and professional skills. Most adults can identify a person who, at some time in their lives, had a significant, positive influence on them. While some mentoring relationships are formal, with clear goals and regular meetings, most such arrangements are informal, arising spontaneously with friends, relatives, co-workers, or teachers.

At its core, mentoring consists of advice and guidance that a person with experience, skills, and knowledge (the mentor) provides to someone who may be less experienced, unfamiliar with how to approach certain professional situations, and in need of guidance (the protégé or "mentee"). Their interactions often consist of counseling, training, supporting, discussing, and/or instructing over time and in varying contexts. Informal mentoring occurs when a veteran in some field meets someone relatively new to the endeavor and they discover that they have a rapport that would make ongoing communication useful. Formal mentoring occurs when someone new to a profession is assigned to a person who is more experienced, as a way of learning local culture and effective practices.

The problem with many formal mentoring relationships is that they are artificial and often lack the natural growth of relationships that arise on their own. That is where speed mentoring can be beneficial: a method for pairing individuals modeled on speed dating and focused on time-efficient networking, a quick exchange of ideas, and a better match of mentor with mentee.

How it works

Speed mentoring works by setting up a meeting of a number of people who are interested in becoming mentors and a number of people who could benefit from the advice and guidance of these seasoned professionals.

Then, rather than just having them mingle at random, potential mentors and potential mentees are assigned to one another in pairs. In order to avoid awkward silences, they may also be provided with a few suggested questions, just to get the conversation started. Then after a set period, usually five or 10 minutes, a signal is given and each potential mentee rotates to the next potential mentor.

Simply by knowing that they have only a limited time available, those involved in the process tend to focus on the most critical issues immediately. In addition, speed mentoring avoids those difficult situations where mentors are formally assigned and it quickly becomes apparent that the two individuals have little in common and practically no chance of developing a meaningful relationship.

One field where speed mentoring has an immediate application is higher education. According to Colvin and Ashman (2010), "Universities are increasingly seeking alternative approaches to education that supplement traditional classroom learning" (p. 121). Mentoring, and more specifically speed mentoring, can be used in programs from the administrative level to the classroom. For instance, it could be included as part of an orientation program for new department chairs, with more senior and established chairs offering their services to those new to the position.

In addition, it provides an opportunity for institutions to keep valuable administrators who have recently retired actively involved with the college or university and applying their skills where they are needed most. For students, speed mentoring can help them find a better "fit" with someone who can provide professional advice, make contacts that could lead to internships or job offers, and relate concepts learned in courses to real-world situations.

By providing an organized process for participants to pursue a mentoring relationship during a rapid-paced event, speed mentoring also eliminates other problems that often arise in formal mentoring programs. It is both time and cost effective, more likely to lead to successful matches between individuals, and even during the very first series of rapid interviews introduces people to how varied their options for advice and encouragement really are. Like speed dating, it promotes social interactions and can be fun, beneficial, and intellectually stimulating.

Like speed dating, its effects can be life-changing. It may lead to unexpected friendships, professional networks, and lasting relationships that would never otherwise have been possible. Moreover, younger protégés often meet people who were trailblazers in their fields, leaders who can be demanding but supportive, assist them with professional problems, and offer them insights they cannot attain in any other way.

Nevertheless, speed mentoring, like anything done at great speed, only grazes the surface of the possibilities. It does not delve into the complex and detailed issues that sometimes create a barrier for personal progress. For this reason, it is important that one speed mentoring session progresses to a regular series of meetings where the two people solidify their relationship and continue to provide mutual benefits. Daloz (1999) notes that "as teachers, we have a lot to say about the conditions under which our students may find power, but we must remember that the power itself is theirs" (p. 182).

Mentees discover that their goals are being taken seriously and that their doubts, dilemmas, and conflicts arising in work and life have potential solutions or at least do not have to be faced alone. Mentors receive satisfaction from being able to use their experience for something extremely useful. They often become more invigorated by their contact with younger people who need the benefits of their insights in order to succeed. In other words, it is not only the mentee who comes away from these sessions with valuable resources and support.

"Being able to support students, reapplying concepts in their own lives and developing connections themselves" (p. 127) are three main themes that mentors expressed in a study conducted by Colvin and Ashman (2010). For all these reasons, the office organizing speed mentoring should not assume that its responsibilities are over once the initial "match meeting" has concluded. It will be necessary to follow up with everyone involved, inquiring how matters are progressing and whether continued contact is actually taking place. Speed mentoring should be seen as a stepping-stone into a more extended process. Again, like speed dating, speed mentoring is not the relationship itself but, rather, the process that makes the ongoing relationship possible.

Finally, speed mentoring can become part of an institution's retention strategy, both for students and employees alike. It helps bring new members more fully "into the family" and gives them an important contact whenever they have questions and do not know where to turn. Students are more likely to persist at an institution where they gain a sense that someone sincerely cares about them and with whom they can solve minor problems before the problems grow into major disasters. Employees can be cautioned against making the sort of mistakes that are all too common when someone is new to an institution and does not yet fully understand local policies and traditions. Moreover, it helps people who are serving as chair or dean for the first time to "hit the ground running" and tap into the wealth of experience that a suitable mentor can provide.

Administrators and faculty members can experiment with speed mentoring at very low cost and only a small commitment of their own time. It is a process that makes a great deal of sense in times of continued limitations to academic budgets and environments where there is concern about rates of student and employee attrition. Most important, speed mentoring simply works better than traditional approaches to matching a mentor with a mentee. For academic leaders who are constantly challenged with the need to do more with less, it is an initiative for which the benefits far outweigh the limited cost.

References
Colvin, J. and Ashman, M. (2010). Roles, risks, and benefits of peer mentoring relationships in higher education. *Mentoring & Tutoring: Partnership in Learning*, 18(2), 121-134.
Daloz, L. A. (1999). *Mentor: Guiding the journey of adult learners*. San Francisco: Jossey-Bass.

Reprinted from *Academic Leader,* June 2012

CHAPTER 4

•

Development Across Faculty Careers

Making Changes: How Faculty Do It

Maryellen Weimer, PhD

The process of making instructional changes has not been studied much at all—perhaps because it seems like a simple process. We discover a new idea, are persuaded it's something worthwhile, think it's doable, and we do it! But if that's all that's involved, then how do we explain the widespread failure to implement the changes repeatedly documented by research to promote more and better learning? Or, how do we account for the millions of dollars spent by organizations such as the National Science Foundation (NSF) on educational reform that has resulted in few lasting changes?

The process of changing how we teach is more complicated, and research is starting to uncover the reasons why. Some of the most interesting and substantive work is being done in physics, which does mean that the findings are discipline-specific, but as the research team reports, "we expect that these conclusions are more widely relevant." (010110-13)

The findings highlighted here are based on interviews with 35 physics faculty members who were purposefully selected. The sample included faculty from two- and four-year institutions, as well as places offering graduate degrees in physics. The interviews focused on Peer Instruction, an innovation developed by a physicist, Eric Mazur, which is more specific than the general ideas of students learning together, often in groups. Peer Instruction as Mazur developed it involves the following sequence, usually repeated several times during a class session: a short lecture followed by a conceptual multiple-choice question, which students first answer individually, then discuss with a classmate, after which they may revise their answer. This Peer Instruction approach has been the subject of a great deal of research in physics and other STEM fields where it consistently shows positive effects on learning.

The interviews (each an hour in length) solicited information the research team used to answer five questions: 1) How reliable are faculty self-reports of their use of Peer Instruction? 2) When faculty modify Peer Instruction, what components do they describe using, modifying, or abandoning? 3) What do faculty report knowing about Peer Instruction? 4) How do faculty learn about Peer Instruction? 5) Is there a relationship between the method of Peer Instruction exposure and the extent to which an instructor implements components of Peer Instruction? (010110-1-2)

Findings are explained at length in the article. In a nutshell, here's what the interviews revealed: "Faculty self-reported user status of Peer Instruction is not particularly useful in characterizing their actual practice." (010110-7) The team had identified nine defining characteristics of Peer Instruction as developed by Mazur. Some faculty who claimed to be users of the technique reported only using one or two of the nine features. Using their own categorizations, the research team identified less than half of the self-reported users as high users. Quite obviously those using the approach were modifying it. "Faculty do not use certain features that may be essential to the success of Peer Instruction implementation." (010110-8)

"Overall, about half of faculty who reported to be familiar with PI did not indicate awareness of any specific features of PI beyond getting students to work together." (010110-9) This lack of awareness may be explained by how faculty reported learning about it. Fifty-eight percent said they first learned about Peer Instruction via informal discussion with a colleague. About a quarter learned about it through a workshop. Only eight percent first encountered it by reading. The data do not support a conclusive answer to the last question but "they point toward informal discussion and working on an educational research or curriculum development project" as being ways that enhance implementation. (010110-13)

From these findings, the research team draws three conclusions. First, "there are communication gaps in current dissemination efforts." (010110-13) Faculty are learning about Peer Instruction from each other, and that informal passing of information compromises the accuracy of what's being communicated. Said another way, faculty aren't learning about this instructional approach from the sources (books, articles, websites, etc.) that share accurate information about it. Second, faculty are modifying the innovation and need more guidance to do so effectively. Replicating it exactly isn't the point. "We do not view modifications in general as a problem. Faculty teach in a wide variety of settings, with a wide variety of students, local structures, course expectations, etc." (010110-14) But making modifications without guidance does put the outcomes in jeopardy. The research community needs to be more helpful on this front. And finally, "informal social inter-actions among colleagues are a key mechanism of communication about reforms." (010110-14) The change process is a highly social one. The team recommends "promoting and supporting more opportunities for faculty to come together over an extended period of time to learn and support each other in a structured environment." (010110-15)

This is important and excellent work that goes a long way in advancing our understanding of the change process. It's a very specific case in point, but for those of us who work on change agendas with faculty across disci-plines, the findings ring true.

Reference
Dancy, M., Henderson, C., and Turpen, C., (2016). How faculty learn about and implement research-based instructional strategies: The case of Peer Instruction. *Physical Review Physics Education Research, 12,* 010110

Reprinted from *The Teaching Professor,* May 2016

From a Teaching Assistant to a Teaching Professor

Muhammad A. Khan

Running undergraduate tutorials and labs is a component of graduate students' training at most departments in North American universities. The experience is meant to prepare graduate students for the transition into academia, if they wish (and are fortunate enough to land a position), and to help departments manage teaching loads. TAs typically deliver material provided by the course instructor, help students better understand course concepts, invigilate quizzes and exams, and grade exams and homework assignments. How big is the change when a TA transitions from providing support to teaching the course? Earlier this year, I found out firsthand.

I'm ABD in a department of mathematics and statistics that has a program that allows a few graduate students to run first-year mathematics courses as instructors of record. I was lucky enough to be selected for this program, and although I had some previous teaching experience, being entirely responsible for a course was a big change. I found it exciting and challenging. Based on my experiences, I'd like to summarize what I've learned and share it with you as advice—but first a bit about the biggest differences.

The most obvious difference in my case was class size; 40 students in my tutorials, 250 in my course. The second and subtler difference involved added responsibilities. No longer can you cover some of the key ideas like you could in the tutorial setting. My course was one section of a multisection coordinated course, which meant I had to keep pace with everyone else. In addition, I had the new responsibility of setting up the assignments and preparing the exams. I wondered what I would do if the midterm turned out to be a disaster. Could I gauge the degree of difficulty needed for the final? Finally, there is the small matter of student evaluations. You really don't want to fall below the department average, do you?

- *Take center stage:* Don't be alarmed—I understand the importance of moving towards learner-centered classrooms rather than teacher-dominated ones. To me, taking charge is not the same as dictating what happens in class. The students are looking to the teacher to maintain a productive learning environment, and they will follow your lead. Taking a back seat on the assumption it needs to be a participatory classroom can quickly result in students losing focus, especially when there are more than a hundred of them.

- *Break the cycle:* "Write, Wipe, Speak, Repeat," or, as it goes in today's multimedia classrooms, "Click, Click, Click, Repeat." Always going through the content the same way becomes repetitive quickly. Students get bored and struggle to listen. Avoid the monotony by trying something different every now and then. For example, once while teaching geometry, I mentioned the novel *Flatland: A Romance of Many Dimensions*, which describes a flat world where circles, triangles, and squares live. Referring to the novel's plot helped me get my point across, but it also caused some excitement in the classroom.

- *Lesson planning:* The idea of planning instruction is underrated in STEM classes. Maybe it's underrated in all kinds of courses. Most TAs (and a lot of professors) think that lecturing is about trying to cover as much material as possible and then picking up from where you left off next time. I could not disagree more. Following a pre-planned and systematic lesson plan is the way forward. Personally, I use the BOPPPS (bridge, objective, pre-assessment, participatory learning, post-assessment, summary) model. The *bridge* is what gets students hooked to the lesson and is followed by stating the *objective*. *Pre-assessment* gives the instructor an idea how well prepared the students are. I also use it to gauge students' understanding of previous material. *Participatory learning* takes up most of the time, and *post-assessment* provides feedback on the success of the lesson in achieving its objective(s). A *summary* reiterates the key ideas.

- *Rubrics:* TAs and teachers alike face backlash when grading is strict and not uniform. When you're the professor in charge, students come to you with their objections. Transparency is the best way to address grading issues. I recommend creating detailed rubrics for each assignment, posting them online well in advance, and sticking to them when you're grading. It behooves new teachers to consult with other professors if they don't have much experience developing grading criteria for rubrics.

- *Establish multiple lines of communication:* Grading issues highlight the importance of communicating with students, and not just by answering questions during class sessions. Our various learning management systems make communicating with students easy. I post updates on the weekends outlining the activities of the week ahead and then send an email that directs students to these updates.
- *Reflection and receptivity:* Finally, remember you're a new teacher, and all teachers, even experienced ones, make mistakes. The important thing is to learn from them. Feedback from students, peers, and the department head can help identify areas for improvement if it's considered with an open mind. Feedback can also alleviate fears. What you may think is a problem may not even be mentioned in the feedback. Positive student comments build confidence and increase your commitment to becoming the best possible teacher.

Reprinted from *The Teaching Professor,* January 2017

How Can I Engage Adjunct Online Faculty in Professional Development?

B. Jean Mandernach, PhD

The reality for many campuses today is that they're offering an increasing number of online courses and the full-time faculty simply can't teach the number of courses being offered. As a result, more and more adjunct faculty are being hired to help cover these new online courses. The good news is adjuncts offer a lot of benefits. They're much more mobile. They offer a lot of scheduling flexibility to add classes as needed or to cancel classes that aren't needed. Not only are they economically advantageous for the university, but from a student's point of view, the research shows us that adjuncts offer a good perspective that students don't always get from those that are full-time academics.

While there's a lot of advantages of doing this, there are also challenges. How do we best serve this faculty population? What can we do to ensure that our adjunct faculty that teach online are doing so in the best way possible and maximizing the learning experience for our students?

When we think about our traditional faculty development—the things we do to help support faculty—at most universities, this is done with the full-time faculty in mind. Because they're full-time faculty, we assume if they need the help, they're going to come get it. We schedule sessions and interactive events during the times that they're on campus. Typically, it's a very centralized experience. Faculty development comes out of some centralized administrative unit that serves all campus-based faculty.

But when we start thinking about what happens as we increase our number of adjunct faculty, it really challenges this model because the faculty not only are not necessarily on campus, but they're everywhere. And they're on different schedules, they're in different time zones, they have different levels of commitment to the institution, and they have different levels of motivation for engaging in this development. When we start thinking of all these differences, it becomes important that we take a close look at what are we doing to support our adjunct faculty teaching online.

The two inherent differences that we typically think of are status—whether they're part-time or full-time—and that they're teaching online. What we rarely think about is how these two things interact with each other to produce unique considerations that make it a challenge to effectively serve both populations simultaneously.

The obvious consideration is time. When do we do this? For most universities, faculty development personnel are there during traditional eight-to-five office hours. They're there when full-time faculty are there. But adjunct faculty are not typically there during your traditional Monday through Friday workday. Even if they are available on a traditional Monday through Friday workday, they might not even be in the same time zone. We don't know what modes they necessarily want to be reached in. We don't know what skill sets they bring. And they don't necessarily have a connection or a reason to even engage in this faculty development programming.

Add to this that the online student population is different. Oftentimes, it's an older population—a nontraditional population. The term length can be completely different for online classes versus face-to-face classes. The expectations for online teachers can be very different. Sometimes they don't get their class schedule until two or three days before the term begins. The standard of expectations for those teaching online might be very different. And this doesn't even touch on the fact that the technology and the teaching techniques that they need might be vastly different from anything that they've been used to.

So, when we start taking all of this variability into consideration, it's important that we really focus on: what do we need to do for this particular population—not only for adjunct faculty who have a host of issues we need to think about, but for online faculty. When they're adjunct faculty teaching online, how do we best serve them with our faculty development programming? What we need to discuss, then, is the who, what, when, where, why, how, and what you can do at your institution to support your adjunct faculty teaching online.

Let's start with the "who." The first thing you need to do is clearly think about: who am I trying to reach with any given faculty development initiative? In some cases, it might only be the adjunct faculty. In some cases, it might be relevant to all faculty whether they're full-time or adjunct. Sometimes it's online only. Sometimes it's all faculty. Sometimes it might only be specific to one course or one department. Other times, maybe, it's only your new faculty.

If you want adjunct online faculty to attend, they need to know that the programming is targeting them. They need to be invited. We can't make assumptions that they know what they need or that they know what's good for them. So, when you're thinking about, what am I making; first of all, identify who is the target population? Then the second thing is, invite that target population. Tell them it's for them. If it's for adjunct only who are brand new to teaching online, those individuals need to be selected, targeted, and invited. And it needs to be very clear to them that that's who this faculty development initiative is for.

Research tells us adjunct faculty typically don't understand the institutional culture, and they receive a lot of emails that they don't need. So, the result of this is they get into "delete mode." All these things are coming in, delete, delete, delete, delete. They need to know that this one is actually for them, that it targets them, that the initiative that you're doing is going to be uniquely relevant to their needs.

The first consideration—you need to target it to the audience and invite the intended audience. If you want faculty to attend, they have to know that it's for them and that they will benefit from that faculty development initiative.

The second thing you must think about is the "what." What are we doing faculty development on? There's a lot of levels to take into consideration. At the institutional level, we often don't think about what our adjunct remote faculty are going to need, because campus-based faculty don't need this at all. They understand the institutional culture. They understand the institutional timeline, the expectations, the various systems, and they even know the acronyms.

Adjunct faculty don't always know this information, and that challenge is compounded when they're remote and may not even be familiar with the physical campus. So, you have to think about: what institutional factors are they going to need information about? Then think about what pedagogical factors are going to be unique for someone who maybe doesn't have experience, not only with online teaching, but with college teaching in general.

And then, what technical considerations are going to be important to allow them to be effective? At a minimum, this includes things like knowing which systems they use for which things; ensuring they have access to all the different systems they're going to need. Email and the learning management system are obvious ones, but what about things for grade challenges, or for helping students with disabilities, or for grade challenges that are for specific populations such as athletes or other unique circumstances at the institution? Adjunct faculty don't know these hoops. Remote faculty aren't aware of the various avenues they can go for assistance. We need to think about what those individuals will need.

There are also practical considerations. Do they even know where to go for help? Do they know what avenues are open to them and available to them? And are we connecting with them on the levels they need? Are we even telling them who else teaches that course, and who they can go to for course-specific questions?

In the department, adjunct online teaching faculty are often hired by an online learning program and may not have a connection to the department. They need to know who in that department do they report to? Who is responsible for their evaluations? Who's responsible for scheduling, or for grade challenges, or other things? We need to be much more explicit when we talk about faculty development programming, because they simply don't know the context.

It's like they always say, "you don't know what you don't know." Adjunct remote faculty are often left very blind, not sure what they're missing, or who they need to ask, or where they go to get the necessary information. The key here is to give them what they need. They want "right now, right on" knowledge and skills, so you need to tell them, "Here are the avenues that you need to go to do your job, and to do your job effectively."

When becomes a hard challenge for working with the remote faculty as well. There are two primary routes you can use. Asynchronous routes—in which you just put information out there, online typically, and they can use it at their own discretion—and synchronous—in which you give them immediate interaction, because we're all online at the same time.

Notice with both of those examples, I said "online" because you can't fall into the trap of going back to what you've always done and having campus-centered programming. Even if you have campus-centered programming where you stream it on the Internet, it is not the same as having programming for those that are not on the campus. You have to think about how they would want to interact with this information, what is going to be meaningful, convenient, and engaging.

You also must start expanding *when* you're willing to do your programming. Our research found that most adjuncts were the most interested in programming that happened after 8:00 pm because they were done with their full-time jobs, they were done with their family obligations, and they finally had time to do it.

When we were looking at what day of the week was most effective, what we found was this: there isn't one. What faculty said is, "I need some variability. There is no perfect day to do this, so if you're going to offer synchronous things that require me to be there, you're going to need to do it at night, and you're going to need to give me options on various days." The only two days we found that faculty were not interested in engaging were Friday and Saturday.

We must keep the population in mind. Because they are adjunct faculty, chances are they're working in other capacities, whether that's working in multiple adjunct capacities or in full-time roles, while doing this on the side. Either way, the time that they have available is going to be very limited, so we have to adjust our schedule to make it amenable to when they're available to us.

The other consideration with scheduling is thinking about the term length itself. Online classes are often accelerated. So, if you offer several faculty development programming initiatives early in the semester, and then there's a second accelerated session or a second eight-week term, there might be new faculty that were not even employed at the university the first time around. So, you need to think about the term at which online courses are offered, and then repeat your faculty development programming.

Adjunct appointments are not continuous, so we can't assume that because we offered it in the spring, or because we offered it earlier in the year, that if they were interested they would have attended. The adjunct population can continually shift, so it becomes very, very important that we give them a lot of different opportunities.

Overwhelmingly, the research tells us: utilize asynchronous whenever possible. Synchronous is incredibly challenging with a remote population. And while the faculty reported to us that they would love to attend synchronous events, the reality is, they can't. So, no matter how motivated they are now, and how much they desire interacting in that live kind of capacity, their schedules simply don't allow it. So, utilize asynchronous when you can, and utilize synchronous when you have to. If you're going to utilize synchronous, be sure you do it on multiple occasions, and multiple opportunities to reach as many faculty as possible.

We've already talked about the difference between asynchronous and synchronous, but I think you also need to think about *where*, because just because you say "asynchronous" doesn't actually tell us what that means—whether that is all online, whether it's in the learning management system, whether there's time limits that tell them when to interact, or whether it's just a resource that's always available to them.

We found faculty tend to like time-limited asynchronous faculty development events. They want to interact with others, so they like to know that the material is fresh, that there is going to be somebody there, that there is going to be somebody responding to their questions. But they also don't have unlimited time available. So, for example, you could offer a four-week course that lasts an entire month and asks them to interact several times. Or you could offer it over two weeks and just say, "Over the next two weeks, we're going to interact on this one topic, and then we're going to have a different event for another topic."

The faculty tell us that they would much rather have multiple opportunities for short, time-limited events. They like the synchronous, but they like it more when it's interactive. They typically tell us, "if you're going to have me sign on live to just listen to you, I would have rather you recorded it and let me listen to it on my own." But if it's truly an interactive, engaging event, then they do enjoy the synchronous when their schedules allow it. They also request that you archive those events because even if they miss out on things they want to know, they can go back and participate in those things, or at least receive the information later.

If you really want to maximize your resources, prioritize the time-limited asynchronous first. And once you've created those, if you have additional time, and energy, and staffing available, then move into some of the synchronous programming options. Your rates of attendance will be higher in the asynchronous simply because their schedules allow it. They enjoy interacting with others. So if you start to combine this with what we know about the targeted audience—if you can even have asynchronous events that are for specific disciplines, or for specific courses if you have enough courses offered—the more it connects to what they're doing right now, hands-on and applied, the more likely they are to engage and participate.

You also should think about why your remote faculty would participate. In most cases, we go back to, "well, we have knowledge that they need, and we're going to teach them things. We're going to teach them about their content or about their pedagogy. We're going to give them something about technology." But with the adjunct remote faculty, you also need to think about the bigger picture. Why they engage is often to connect with people at the college. In some cases, they've never even seen the campus; they've never met another faculty member that works there. So, they'll engage in this faculty development as a means of becoming part of that academic institution. So, when you're developing the program, not only should you think about what they need to know and what skills they need to have, but also, how we can give them that in a way that fosters relationships and fosters the connection to the institution.

Not only do adjuncts report that they like connecting with other faculty members, but the research shows that they're much more likely to stay at the institution if they feel a connection with that institution, which in the long-term is going to benefit not only your students, but—from an economic point of view—the institution, by not having to continually bring in new adjunct faculty.

When you start to develop it then, you need to think about holistic programming. You want to give them something they need, the cognitive, technical aspects. But don't forget the psychosocial as well, allowing them to build relationships and connect to the institution. One of the things that we found faculty really enjoyed was being sent a university sweatshirt. They told us, "I felt like I was part of the group." It wasn't that the sweatshirt was magical, although I'm sure that was nice, but it was feeling like they were part of the institution. The fact that they had the sweatshirt with the name on it allowed them to feel connected to that remote, distinct campus that perhaps they've never even been to.

You also want to think about the philosophy. Often when we talk about adjunct faculty, it's *us* teaching *them*. We recognize that they are working professionals and experts in their field, and so we want to teach them all about higher education, we want to teach them about pedagogy. But if you want them to really engage, you need to make it inclusive. You need to bring them in as experts, asking them: What do you do really well? How can you help us teach other people? How can you help mentor us? What programming do you need?

And then think about how this comes into the whole big picture. We can't forget that adjunct faculty are hired simply to teach a course. They're not paid for doing service. They're not paid for doing research. They're paid to teach a course. If we want them to engage with us, it must be because it's important to them.

Rarely are we going to have the resources to be able to pay them for participation, but sometimes they can be rewarded in other ways. Through awards—just getting recognition from the university, perhaps scheduling priority, receiving textbooks, receiving other resources. It's also important to think about how we can integrate them, so they don't feel like this is something else that is being pushed out and required to do without compensation, through building a culture and creating a community of adjunct remote faculty where they're interacting with each other, interacting with the programming, and feeling like that interaction has value to them as a teacher.

You need to create a community-driven event. When they feel invested, not only in the outcome, but in the process itself—the development of topics, doing needs assessments, talking to them about what works and what doesn't, or simply asking them what schedule is most amenable to theirs; they need to feel like they're part of that larger community, and connecting them with others in that community works as a support resource.

If you want to engage the faculty, there are just three things you must remember. Give them good content. Make it holistic content that's relevant to their needs, that's applied, that's timely for what they do. Make sure it's given to them in a manner they can access and use. You can give the best programming ever, but if they can't see it because it's during their scheduled job, they're never going to use it. And you must engage them so they want to use this information, so they want to connect with other faculty, and see a personal value in doing so. As you start to create this kind of environment then, you can start to see them not only has "just adjuncts," which is what some of my faculty used to say, but as valuable parts of the community— valuable faculty members who simply happen to work part-time. By bringing them in as experts, having them advise and serve in different kinds of roles within the adjunct community, they will find the resources that you create are valuable to them and their role.

The key components to bring them in are as follows: make them feel valued, get them invested, and get them involved. When they start to feel valued, invested, and involved, you're going to start to build that culture, that community in which they're part of your institution regardless of the fact that they work remotely, and that they are working from their own homes.

As you start to do this, it's not a matter of the magical faculty development initiative. It's building a culture, giving them good resources, communicating with them so that you're meeting their needs, and then giving them the information in a way they can use and that they can access and interact with in a meaningful fashion.

Adapted from the Magna 20-minute Mentor program "How Can I Engage Adjunct Online Faculty in Professional Development?" July 2005

Adjunct Professional Development Improves Teaching, Builds Community

Rob Kelly

The Department of Behavioral Sciences at St. Louis Community College-Meramec is a diverse department with 16 full-time and 53 adjunct faculty. In an effort to connect those adjuncts to the department, Darlaine Gardetto and some of her colleagues created an adjunct professional development program based on Bloom's Taxonomy.

The department is home to seven disciplines—three career programs and four general disciplines—which has been a challenge in terms of creating a sense of community. Before Gardetto became chair, there had not been any professional development for those part-time instructors, and community-building efforts were ineffective.

The need to improve professional development came from the college's relatively low scores on academic rigor as measured by the Community College Survey of Student Engagement (CCSSE). There was much debate as to why the college had low academic rigor scores and whether they accurately reflected reality. Nevertheless, Gardetto decided to seek ways to intellectually engage the faculty on issues related to it.

Because of the department's reliance on adjunct instructors, Gardetto made it a point to invite them to teaching seminars held over the lunch hour, but they didn't attend. So she and several colleagues decided to start offering weekend workshops for adjuncts, which drew about half of them. And it blossomed, to the point where the department now holds three or four sessions per year.

These workshops typically run approximately four hours and focus on Bloom's Taxonomy, including the following topics:

- Moving multiple-choice exams beyond memorization, using Bloom's Taxonomy
- Creating a philosophy of teaching statement
- Teaching *Generation WTF*

These workshops are popular with the adjuncts because many are used to teaching at surrounding universities as well and have struggled to maintain academic rigor at the community college level without losing students or taking a hit on their students' evaluations of their teaching.

"Teaching at the community college is somewhat different than teaching at our local private universities. They would try to use the same syllabus that they were using at the university and it wouldn't work. Their initial thought was that the students weren't up to doing the job and would end up watering down the curriculum so they wouldn't have students fail. They were interested in discussing the ways they could integrate Bloom's Taxonomy into their teaching to ramp up their rigor but at the same time not lose their students," Gardetto says.

Gardetto and the other workshop coordinators come up with topics and provide short readings to generate interest and to prepare instructors to participate.

In each workshop, part of the time faculty meet as a department and part of the time they work in groups according to discipline, an approach used both for full- and part-time faculty development. "When I became chair, my experience with this department had been that our disciplinary boundaries were not recognized, and that was not a good thing for us. The idea had been that we'd see ourselves as more of a community if we were part of a big department. But I think, in fact, what happened was that we didn't feel as connected because college professors are connected through their disciplines ... I think they really are hungry for intellectual community and for recognition of themselves as professors within a discipline," Gardetto says.

This sense of community is evident in the instructors' investment in the workshops. In addition to taking time on Saturdays to participate, many instructors want to have more control over what happens in the workshops. For example, at a recent workshop, the facilitators gave a presentation and then the instructors wanted to have a discussion about the assignments in their courses. A next step will be a symposium where part-time instructors will do presentations for each other. To that end, the department has set up a Blackboard site to enable instructors to maintain the dialogue beyond the workshops.

The challenge now is to figure out how to direct the enthusiasm these part-time instructors are putting into their professional development. "They want more control over the content of those Saturday workshops, which is very interesting. That's a sign that the community is working and that they're coming together and want to empower their lives," Gardetto says.

The key to the success of this adjunct development is the participation of the full-time faculty. "It really has to be faculty driven. Faculty need to step up to the plate to do this. And it's such satisfying work. I can't think of anything that's more interesting, other than teaching, than interacting with colleagues and helping with their professional development. So much of the professional development—at least on our campus—is run by people who are in staff and administrative positions. Faculty need to be doing this, because they're the ones who are trained in the disciplines," Gardetto says.

Reprinted from *Academic Leader,* April 2012

Strategic HR Approaches to Building and Sustaining a Diverse Adjunct Workforce

Alvin Evans and Edna Chun, DM

With nontenure-track faculty now comprising 70 percent of the faculty workforce, academic leaders face daunting challenges in creating proactive workplace strategies that address this new reality. Even though more than a quarter of nontenure-track faculty are now in full-time nontenure-track appointments, the majority still teach part-time. Despite the urgency of addressing this dramatic shift in the faculty workforce, as we point out in *Creating a Tipping Point: Strategic Human Resources in Higher Education* (Jossey-Bass, 2013), higher education has been comparatively slow to realize the potential of human resources (HR) in developing strategic talent practices. By contrast, in the private sector, a 20-year research study (Ulrich et. al., 2008) with 40,000 respondents in 441 companies found that when HR professionals develop high-performance work systems, these practices affect 20 percent of business results. Such practices, however, need to be integrated and systematic to produce these outcomes.

A major difficulty arises in higher education due to the typical organizational structure of HR. HR tends to be viewed almost exclusively as a staff function, generally reports to the chief financial officer, and usually only has responsibility for certain faculty functions such as benefits and retirement. Academic affairs often also houses an academic personnel function, and this bifurcation between academic and staff personnel can be problematic in terms of the development of talent strategies that serve the entire institution. In the new millennium, however, HR needs to work collaboratively with academic affairs to redesign its practices and move from transaction-based, siloed operations to proactive, strategic workforce approaches that build and sustain the adjunct faculty workforce.

In this article, we address two architectural elements of a cohesive talent strategy for adjunct faculty in which HR can add significant value: 1) talent acquisition through recruitment, outreach, and hiring and 2) talent development through a state-of-the-art total rewards strategy.

The first step is to understand the current demographic profile of adjunct faculty. Recent research by Paul Yakoboski of the TIAA-CREF Institute finds that two-thirds work in public institutions and are somewhat evenly spread among institutional types. Yet approximately 70 percent of the community college workforce serves in adjunct appointments. Further, as Yakoboski notes, the average age of adjunct faculty is skewed toward older individuals, with 71 percent over the age of 40. In terms of race and ethnicity, 2014–15 data from the National Center for Education Statistics indicates that of the 529,832 part-time instructional faculty, nearly three-fourths are white (38 percent white women, 35 percent white men), 5.4 percent are Hispanic, 7.8 percent are African American, and 4.2 percent are Asian American.

At the same time, we know that the student body is becoming increasingly diverse in terms of racial/ethnic diversity as well as in the enrollment of older nontraditional students, part-time students, and low-income and first-time-in-college students. From the standpoint of racial and ethnic diversity, between 1976 and 2012, the percentage of white students has declined from 84 percent to 60 percent, while the percentage of minority students has more than doubled. Given this rapidly changing demographic profile, greater diversity is needed among adjunct faculty to create a more representative faculty workforce, provide role models in the classroom, and prepare students for citizenship and careers in a global society. As a result, we now focus on specific ways that HR professionals can work collaboratively with academic leaders to build a sustainable and diverse adjunct talent pipeline and promote greater inclusion of adjunct faculty in the mainstream of campus life.

Talent acquisition

One of the primary barriers to building a pipeline of diverse and talented adjuncts is the nature of the hiring process. Adjunct hiring usually occurs on an as-needed basis as departments determine the level of enrollment in courses. This decentralized, just-in-time approach that usually takes place through direct appointments by department chairs often has been driven by budgetary cutbacks that have forced academic departments to rely more heavily on a contingent workforce. While speed and efficiency are important, Jennifer Ruth and Michael Berube in their new book, *The Humanities, Higher Education, and Academic Freedom: Three Necessary Arguments* (Palgrave McMillan, 2015) argue that such ad hoc hiring processes would benefit from greater professionalization. Without a systematic hiring process and formalized criteria, they note that adjunct hiring can result in a kind of patronage when these "at will" faculty members owe their employment to whomever is the department head at the time.

To address both the professionalization and diversification of the adjunct hiring pipeline, HR can help promote greater consistency by partnering with academic leaders in the following ways:

- Analyze jobs in terms of required and preferred qualifications and competencies that align with educational mission and disciplinary goals
- Develop effective sourcing and outreach strategies to attract diverse talent
- Build diverse adjunct pools and advance screening for minimum qualifications
- Define the stages of the adjunct hiring process
- Develop relevant hiring guidelines
- Ensure time-sensitive appointments

Because of the predominance of adjunct faculty, HR departments in community colleges tend to have developed more systematic guidelines and resources, such as the Los Rios Community College District in California that offers a well-developed set of practices and resources (*www.losrios.edu/hr/Recruitment/hiringadjunctfaculty.html#Other_helpful_resources*). As an example from a private research university, Drexel University's HR department offers the opportunity to work with HR business partners in recruiting adjuncts as well as provides a systematic presentation of the workflow (*http://drexel.edu/hr/atDrexel/employmentOps/adjuncts/*).

Total rewards strategy and talent development

Developing a cohesive total rewards strategy for adjunct faculty is a critical approach to retaining talent. A comprehensive approach to both direct and indirect compensation will create a cohesive system aligned with institutional goals that includes the design of competitive compensation programs, benefits, and retirement plans as well as work/life offerings, recognition and award programs, and professional development opportunities.

According to recent salary surveys, the median salary of adjunct professors is $2,700 per semester course and ranges from an average of $20,000 to $25,000 per year. This relatively low level of pay requires careful institutional analysis in addressing adjunct retention and job satisfaction in light of available budgetary resources. HR professionals can assist in evaluating the value proposition for adjunct faculty by conducting benchmarking surveys that assess market position in relation to peer institutions and by developing salary recommendations that address budget realities while maintaining competitive advantage.

On the benefits side of the equation, some institutions have moved to limit adjunct participation in benefit programs under the Patient Protection and Affordable Care Act by capping course loads. Other institutions have created separate benefit programs with higher deductibles that meet the letter of the law but make enrolling in health care a costly proposition. Such policies require careful review and analysis to determine their impact on retaining adjuncts given their need to sustain a viable income and maintain adequate health care for themselves and their families. Furthermore, at many institutions, office hours are not paid, diminishing the ability of adjuncts to work closely with students. These factors suggest the need for an overall evaluation and systematization of the institution's policies and pay practices for adjuncts.

Professional development is another important area in which HR can work with academic leaders and teaching and learning centers to offer leading-edge programs that specifically address the needs of adjuncts. Such programs include, for example, orientation programs that feature several follow-up sessions, discussions of academic policy and available teaching resources, classroom technology and online course development, and work/life seminars. Consideration can be given to providing a stipend for orientation and professional development programs because they fall outside of the adjunct faculty workload.

In today's higher education environment, development of a competitive adjunct talent strategy that optimizes institutional resources while providing greater job satisfaction to part-time faculty is critical to organizational success. The strategic partnership of HR with academic leaders offers the opportunity for the creation of talent approaches that align with educational goals while ensuring the continued contributions of a diverse and talented adjunct faculty workforce.

Reprinted from *Academic Leader,* June 2016

Faculty Fellows Program Provides Incentives, Structure to Improve Teaching

Rob Kelly

Winston-Salem State University recently implemented its Faculty Fellows Program, a comprehensive, two-tiered model of faculty development to serve the diverse needs of tenure-track and tenured faculty members. The program was initiated by the Office of Faculty Affairs under the leadership of Associate Provost Denise Pearson in fall 2012 with a cohort of approximately 40 faculty members.

The goal of the program is to provide structure and incentives to encourage faculty members to improve their pedagogical strategies and to help them plan their career paths. Many of the workshops, which are offered through the Center for Excellence in Teaching and Learning (CETL), are appropriate for all faculty members regardless of rank and are open to all faculty even if they are not in the Faculty Fellows Program. A major goal of the program is to take a systematic approach in which faculty benefit from being in a cohort.

"Whenever you're in a community of teachers and scholars who are talking about teaching and actively working to learn new ways to improve their teaching, I think it's invigorating just to be a part of that conversation," says Tiffany Baffour, director of CETL.

The Faculty Fellows Program focuses on four major topic areas: students, teaching methods and pedagogy, materials and technology, and discipline-specific needs.

Junior Faculty of Distinction

Tenure-track faculty who participate in the Faculty Fellows Program work toward a Junior Faculty of Distinction Certificate. This requires successful completion of at least eight development workshops—four that focus on pedagogy, two on technology, and two activities of the participant's choice, such as being part of a faculty learning community. Faculty can join an existing learning community or create one on a specific topic of interest to them. For example, a group of faculty created an interdisciplinary learning community on qualitative inquiry. This learning community held a series of monthly meetings and plans a full-day symposium for April 2013.

Participants also need to create a career development plan in conjunction with their department chair or faculty member that sets short- and long-term goals for teaching, research, and service.

Some of the workshops are designed specifically for junior faculty members. For example, a recent series focused on branding and professional development among new faculty, providing opportunities for participants to reflect on their area of specialization and what that means for their teaching, research, and service.

In recognition of their commitment to teaching, participants who successfully complete the program receive a $1,000 stipend, a certificate, and a provost-hosted event. Since one of the criteria for promotion and tenure is being able to demonstrate how one has worked to improve one's teaching, faculty have a good incentive to complete the program, Baffour says.

Distinguished Master Teachers

The criteria and incentives for senior faculty are the same as for junior faculty; however, instead of creating a career development plan, senior faculty present a pedagogical workshop or poster presentation at a CETL event on topics such as:

- Assessment of learning
- Course design
- Pedagogy
- High-impact instruction
- Collaborative or cooperative learning
- STEM education
- Teaching inclusively
- Revitalizing/maintaining work-life balance
- General education

Outcomes

Although there has not yet been a formal quantitative assessment of the Faculty Fellows Program, qualitative feedback from the first cohort has been positive. Participants said they found being part of a community that discusses teaching has been helpful and that they like getting feedback from a variety of faculty members.

Several participants of the first group of Distinguished Master Teachers have been really interested and passionate about giving back to CETL. Although it is not required, several participants are conducting workshops with the information they have acquired through the program, a sign that the program has had positive effects on participants.

Baffour is working on implementing ways to formally evaluate the program. Possible techniques include comparing student evaluations before and after participation in the program and intensive interviews with participants. "I'm very interested in getting feedback from the group in terms of what worked well and what didn't work well. ... I'm curious to see how this group feels about the career development plan and whether or not it's useful to them," she says.

Reprinted from *Academic Leader,* April 2013

Team Teaching: Active Learning Practice for Teachers

Karen Sheriff LeVan and Marissa King

Most of us have applauded the various calls for a fuller understanding of active student learning, but long-term classroom change can intimidate teachers. Just like students, teachers need hands-on, feedback-filled practice to improve use of active learning in the classroom. Although team teaching is often seen as too expensive these days, the benefits of this kind of teacher collaboration are unparalleled. Team teaching takes the idea of on-the-job practice to a different level by blurring the lines between our roles as teachers and learners. Team teaching isn't a new idea, and it doesn't replace the articles, lectures, or collegial discussions we use to enlarge our instructional understandings. However, we believe it offers teachers a first-rate active learning experience because that's precisely the experience we had when we joined forces in teaching Basic Writing.

In the planning stage, before students' backpacks and personalities fill the room, professors use their own assumptions to create course structures, fashion assignments, and decide on content. Habits, rarely questioned during solitary walks from office to classroom, sometimes clash when two professors try to finalize class plans. They discover that their perspectives on the success of a class activity aren't the same, and that causes them to have a conversation during which their individual assumptions are examined. Resolution of differences often requires each team member to try new methods or refine old ones, which can feel uncomfortable but leads to professional growth. It happened that way for us. Instead of holding a new method at arms' length, we found ourselves learning from each other during planning as well as in class.

Learning to teach as you're team teaching a course is not at all like getting advice after a colleague has visited your class. In that case, the decision of whether or not to follow the advice is an individual one. In team-taught courses, faculty share power, which means the switch from teacher to learner and back isn't optional; it's automatic. It forces faculty to try the new methods and learn from each other how to execute them effectively.

Even instructors who share teaching philosophies may disagree when they're evaluating an activity's success or deciding what needs to happen next in class. Team-teaching conflicts offer sustained practice that goes beyond a brief observational conversation. Learning, as our students often tell us, can be uncomfortable. Team teaching has forced us to do things we haven't done before and to learn from the experience.

Teaching-learning literature offers a robust conversation about the benefits of team teaching for students, but perhaps we need more focus on how its shared power structure so effectively transforms teachers into learners. As team teachers move separately around the room in a referee-style dance, each inevitably collects different information about what is happening in small groups or independent practice. Gathering more real-time information on student performance can clearly help students if used accurately, but what professors learn from each other needs deeper investigation. In our classrooms, we don't question each other's on-the-spot decisions, but as we teach together, we're forced to acknowledge that, like referees, we don't always see the play in the same way. With two experts in the room, it's difficult to bluff about student learning and even harder to make informed instructional decisions.

Team teaching is harder than it looks but has ongoing benefits. As we work together, we've gotten clearer about the assumptions we're making and the habits that characterize how we teach. We're also finding it easier to move our teaching styles in different directions. Though team teaching requires vulnerability to put work that feels personal in front of colleagues, it offers sustained practice that can't be had from a come-and-go peer review.

Team teaching shouldn't be ruled out automatically because of its costs. When it comes to an effective way to promote the growth and development of individual faculty members, it may be an investment more departments, programs, and institutions should consider. In our cases, it has been one of the most memorably active learning experiences of our careers. We teach differently as a result of having taught together.

Reprinted from *The Teaching Professor,* February 2015

After Promotion and Tenure Maintaining Faculty's Upward Trajectory

N. Douglas Lees, PhD

While a necessary and worthy milestone, earning promotion and tenure is not an end goal of an academic career. During the pre-tenure years, a faculty member is gearing up for growth in the areas (e.g., teaching, research and teaching) defined by the institution to meet the mark for tenure. Ideally, the latter part of the pre-tenure period is one where the quality of the work is on the rise, there is an emerging reputation, and the products (e.g., presentations, exhibitions, publications, proposals for/success in funding) of success are generated at an increased pace. At the time of dossier submission, there should be a record with a definitive upward trajectory. The challenge at this point is to capitalize on the momentum created to begin planning for the next step, the promotion to full professor. This, however, is not the way all cases proceed.

Some faculty members will do what is necessary to earn tenure, but once that goal is achieved, they are comfortable remaining associate professors until they retire. This situation is exacerbated by the fact that the criteria for promotion to full professor tend to be more stringent, which exaggerates initial ambivalence.

Some cultures in higher education seem to support this unfortunate attitude. In fact, a personal experience on my own campus, I am sorry to say, exposed me to such a culture. During a panel discussion with an audience of first-year faculty members, a panelist said, "Avoid doing anything beyond the minimal amount of committee service while pre-tenure; once you achieve tenure you will have plenty of time for that." Diverting attention when a faculty member is energized by a successful application for P&T and at a time when new collaborations are being established, new projects are being launched, and invitations for presentations, keynotes, and the like are beginning to be received seems a disservice to both the faculty member and the institution. To avoid the planned, permanent associate professor, some institutions have a P&T guideline statement that says, in effect, "We should not offer tenure to a faculty member who lacks the ambition or abilities to achieve full professor rank." The problem is this: How do you know?

The focus of this article is on strategies and interventions that help mid- and late-career faculty maintain their momentum beyond tenure and on those effective in the maintaining high productivity of senior faculty. Each case will be different in its manifestations and in any necessary solutions. The individual responsible for monitoring each case, directly or indirectly, is the chair.

Higher education has evolved to monitoring well the progress of pre-tenure faculty. Aside from annual reviews by chairs, they are sometimes subject to annual reappointment reviews with a committee that will ultimately make the first recommendation on tenure. Some institutions have more in-depth third-year reviews in which faculty members receive feedback from a level beyond the department. Finally, mentoring of new faculty is becoming more common. However, once tenure is earned, much of the monitoring disappears, leaving the annual review as the only certain event where faculty progress is evaluated.

During annual reviews with faculty on the brink of tenure or beyond, chairs might consider the following strategies. For the soon-to-be associate professor, the chair might focus on goal setting that raises the bar on previous accomplishments while asking if the faculty member has sufficient resources to achieve the goals. This tells the faculty member that there is both an expectation of greater success and confidence that the faculty member will succeed, while it also acknowledges resource needs the chair can convey.

For those five to 10 years beyond tenure, the chair should carefully monitor productivity for changes in type and decreases in quality because these may be signs of some dissatisfaction with the present portfolio of work or a general loss of enthusiasm. The earlier the detection of declines, the better the chances of reversal. In a case in which a faculty member shows less than optimal productivity over time, the chair might consider asking questions such as, "What would you like to be doing in five years?" If the response is, "What I am doing now," then a follow-up conversation as to possible reasons for reduced productivity is called for. A chair can work with such an individual to address obstacles. However, if the answer is, "I have lost the zeal for competitive research and want to change my career focus to undergraduate teaching or community engagement or administrative service," the chair must embark on a longer, more complex plan of helping to make this happen.

Beyond dealing with individual cases of stalled or subpar performance, strategies and environmental conditions can be employed or created by chairs and deans to help mid- to late-career faculty remain fully engaged and productive. These strategies are based on the research of Bland and Bergquist (1997) on what matters to successful senior faculty.

The research reveals that the number one characteristic responsible for the continued productivity of senior (mid- to late-career) faculty is their internal drive. Anyone who has spent time in a higher education environment will be able to list such faculty; these are the relentless workers who will not be denied success and who find a way around every obstacle. Successful senior faculty members are also well-networked; they know all the top people in the field and are aware of the up-and-comers. In the vernacular, these faculty members are "players." They also have a strong sense of autonomy and are very comfortable espousing their professional opinions even when they depart from the current dogma. In a sense, they are risk-takers. They are also busy people, so they are sensitive to assignments that take time away from their primary work. In addition, as they age, work-life balance becomes increasingly important. Ultimately, as retirement approaches, many focus on their legacy.

Armed with this information, chairs and deans should be able to generate opportunities and conditions that would support many of these characteristics, thereby increasing the likelihood of promoting further productivity from senior faculty. To facilitate networking, the chair could send a faculty member to a conference or invite a new collaborator to visit campus for several days when there would be a symposium, ample time to discuss new projects, and opportunities to meet with students and perhaps teach a class. Sending the faculty to the collaborator would be a variant on the same theme.

Another way to promote networking is to sponsor a conference on campus in the faculty member's area of interest. Depending on a number of factors, some help from the dean may be necessary. To address the autonomy/ risk-taking attribute, the chair could provide resources for a pedagogical experiment the faculty member has wanted to try or to launch a research project that might have a high reward but for which there are no preliminary data to support an external grant proposal. The chair could easily avoid assigning the faculty member to committees where the required expertise is not a good match and generally protect the time of the faculty member. The chair might also avoid assigning classes that interfere with late Wednesday afternoons with grandchildren, for example.

Beyond reinforcing the characteristics of successful senior faculty members, there are some favorable environmental factors identified by senior faculty that a chair can enhance. Having high expectations for faculty performance (e.g., big fish like to "swim, "collaborate with other big fish), a collegial atmosphere, and recognition and rewards for excellent performance are all things on which a chair can have some influence. Chairs should recognize through department and campus venues the contributions of excellent faculty and be prepared to nominate them for appropriate awards. Finally, goal alignment among the institution, the department, and the individual has emerged in surveys as an important factor that keeps senior faculty motivated. Chairs are in a position to ensure at least part of that.

Campuses are realizing that successful associate and full professors are not guaranteed to continue high productivity until retirement. They may need help and attention from time to time in order to reach their potential and for the institution to benefit fully from their capabilities. Chairs will play a critical role in monitoring performance of these individuals. Each case will be unique, from those who are motivated and work productively throughout their careers to those who may get stuck more than once, and chairs will have to employ multiple approaches and utilize a variety of personal skills to be successful.

Reprinted from *Academic Leader,* July 2016

Encouraging Faculty Leadership Development

Rob Kelly

Pareena Lawrence, dean and chief academic officer of Augustana College, says that faculty need to take on a different and more active leadership role in order to meet the demands of the 21st-century higher education landscape. "There is limited space in the traditional system of shared governance to share with faculty leadership the rapid changes in higher education. It seems like sometimes I have a lot of information, but they have to make some of the decisions as part of shared governance without access to much of this information. And there's no committee on campus that's looking at long-term trends or threats that should concern us," she says.

Part of the problem is that institutions are so discipline-based and committees are often task-based, that "it doesn't allow for these conversations to happen with most faculty together such that we can come to joint decisions," Lawrence says.

In addition, there appears to be less of an emphasis on developing faculty leaders than on developing student leaders. "We talk about student leadership. Look at our mission statements. We want students to be leaders. We want them to be adaptable to a changing world. We don't use that language for faculty. We don't say we want our faculty to be leaders. We don't say we want them to be adaptable to a changing world," Lawrence says.

Here are Lawrence's recommendations for encouraging faculty members to get involved in institutional leadership:

- **Be willing to give up power.** Inviting faculty to participate in decision-making means having to give up some control. "You are asking them to come to the table and be leaders. That means in some ways you are giving some of your power away and saying, I want you to share this power with me so we can make better decisions,"

Lawrence says. "Some administrators are not comfortable with sharing or willing to share this decision-making authority with faculty members. Do you really want to do this?"

- **Have an agenda.** When providing leadership opportunities, start by asking, What will be the end result? What do we want out of it? "Each campus and each leader has to decide what they want to come from developing faculty leaders. Do you want better curricular decisions? Do you want faculty to consider innovative programs? Do you want faculty leaders to understand the budget of the college? Then you build a program toward that," Lawrence says.

- **Be sure everybody understands his or her responsibilities.** Each committee member and its chair, and each department chair needs to understand his or her responsibilities. "One of the things we're working on is making sure that committee and department chairs understand what it means to be chair," Lawrence says. "[Often,] department chairs learn from their predecessors because there's no formal program. If we have a great department chair who models great chairship, we aspire to be like that person. If you have a person who is laissez-faire, you may end up with someone who does not pay much attention because that's how it was done in their department in the past. Department chairs need to be equipped to take on this role and the expectations of their positions must be made clear to them as they change and unfortunately expand. What do good department chairs do? Not, what did your predecessor do?

  "Each committee needs to understand its charge and how members operate together. What is the agenda? What does the core curriculum committee need to know about the tasks and timelines of the educational policy committee? We need to spend at least a couple hours with the committee members and chairs at the beginning of the year going over the charge and talking about what is expected of the committee this year," Lawrence says.

- **Build trust.** When Lawrence became dean, the main goal of her first year was to build trust among the faculty. Part of building trust involves being clear about your leadership style. "My first year [was focused on] investing in those relationships so faculty [would] know how I function. ... If you don't have their trust, nothing else you do matters. You can do all the agenda setting, follow all the rules, but if you haven't built that sense of trust you won't get them to participate and be willing to look for answers [and] to problem solve with you," Lawrence says.

- **Seek diverse participation.** When forming a task force, make sure that you don't always select the same people to participate; avoid the impression that there are a select few worthy of participating in decision-making.
- **Be clear on the decision-making process.** Different decisions call for different processes. "Do you like making decisions yourself? Do you just want recommendations from the faculty and not joint decisions? Sometimes I only want recommendations because the ultimate call is mine. Sometimes it's really a joint decision. When you call them to the table and ask for input and if it's perceived that you are not taking that input in, if the decision is already made and you're doing this for a show, they'll know soon enough. It may take a year. It may take two years, and then you're not going to have people show up. Why would they?"

Reprinted from *Academic Leader,* March 2013

Best Practices in Preparing Academic Leaders

Jeffrey L. Buller, PhD

It's increasingly common for colleges and universities to offer programs designed to help chairs, deans, and other academic administrators become more effective. Sometimes falling under a center for teaching and learning, at other times existing as an independent office for leadership and professional development, these programs reflect the recognition that college administrators often come to their jobs woefully underprepared for what their responsibilities will be. These leadership development programs are well-intentioned efforts to "backfill" the skills needed by academic leaders who, although they may be experts in their disciplines, know very little about how to make an academic unit function effectively.

But how can institutions know whether their academic leadership initiatives are worth the resources they require? Here are five practices commonly followed by successful leadership training programs that can help institutions establish or improve opportunities for administrators to succeed.

1. **Academic leadership programs should include training in both highly specialized day-to-day responsibilities and more global administrative issues.** Administrators need to know how to develop and implement budgets, conduct effective meetings, write evaluation reports, submit equipment requests, and engage in a wide variety of other activities that are basic to their jobs. If they don't know how to mediate a personnel conflict, they're not likely to have the skills they need to make their programs run smoothly. But their programs won't run smoothly if these specific tasks are <u>all</u>

they know. Academic leaders also have to reflect on their leadership philosophy, know where management ends and leadership begins, handle the stress of their positions, think about the future in creative and visionary ways, and understand how they fit into the larger picture of higher education globally. Effective academic leadership programs cover all points on this spectrum. They include sessions on how to write effective résumés but also on the strategies of servant leadership. They don't ignore programs on developing effective notices for position vacancies, but neither do they limit their programs to explaining policies and software. Good academic leadership programs address both the forest and the trees because an effective administrator cannot afford to ignore either one.

2. **Academic leadership programs should be both scaffolded and continuous.** Although the types of workshops we just considered are essential to any academic leadership program, workshops alone do not make a program. A series of workshops, no matter how excellent the topics may be, rarely change someone's behavior. Academic leaders begin to see their administrative processes improve when programs are scaffolded (introductory sessions lead to intermediate sessions, which lead to advanced sessions) and continuous (there is follow-up, either in person or electronically, between sessions so that progress doesn't stop at the end of the workshop). Just as an academic course is more than a number of discrete lessons on isolated topics, so are effective leadership programs carefully structured sequences that build on one another and reinforce the ideas that have been covered.

3. **Academic leadership programs should include projects.** Another way in which leadership programs should be like courses is that they need to require homework. If you've ever audited a course, you know that your level of understanding the material is far less than if you actually enroll in the course and complete all the assignments, papers, and tests. Academic leadership programs are similar. Participants need to apply the information they cover and the skills they develop in activities that benefit their institutions. Projects serve as a way of evaluating the degree to which the participants have mastered the material and of continuing the scaffolded and continuous nature of the program described earlier. If people don't apply what they've learned in the program by engaging in a meaningful project, much of the program's content remains merely theoretical to them and has little effect on their administrative practices.

4. **Academic leadership programs should include discussion and support groups.** All academic leaders face challenges from time to time. They need an opportunity to discuss these challenges with people who may be having similar experiences and who aren't their supervisors. Many participants in academic leadership programs say that the networking opportunities these programs provide are their most valuable feature. They help the participants realize that they're not alone in the problems they're having and that they're not necessarily doing anything wrong when things don't work out according to plan. Even experienced academic leaders may be reluctant to talk about their problems to their bosses for fear that they'd be admitting weakness or failure. Discussion and support groups alleviate that fear because they offer an element of peer-to-peer consolation and consultation.

5. **Academic leadership programs should include appropriate forms of assessment.** A series of workshops that merely provide administrators a chance to get together from time to time, venting and discussing interesting ideas, may be a pleasant activity, but it doesn't achieve its fundamental goal: improving administrative performance. Assessment activities should include self-reflection (what have I done differently as a result of this program?), supervisor evaluation (how has the participant's performance improved as a result of this program?), and stakeholder insight (how has your colleague or supervisor's performance changed as a result of this program?). This assessment helps those in charge of the program monitor the effectiveness of their activities and alerts them to changes that need to be made.

Reprinted from *Academic Leader,* September 2015

About the Contributors

Kenneth L. Alford, PhD, is a professor of church history and doctrine at Brigham Young University. After serving almost 30 years on active duty in the U.S. Army, he retired as a Colonel in 2008. Ken served in numerous assignments while on active military duty, including the Pentagon, eight years teaching computer science at the United States Military Academy at West Point, and four years as department chair and professor teaching strategic leadership at the National Defense University in Washington, DC. He has published and presented on a wide variety of topics during his career.

Alan Altany is the director of the Center for Teaching, Learning and Scholarship at Georgia Southern University.

Kami Barrett-Batchelder, MPA, MA, serves as the associate director of public relations/community outreach for Osher Lifelong Learning Institute at Florida Atlantic University. Outside of work, Barrett is involved in several organizations which include Public Relations Society of America, Northern Palm Beaches Cultural Alliance, and PRN Networking. Barrett currently is pursuing her PhD in adult/community education from Florida Atlantic University. She got her MS in public administration also from Florida Atlantic University.

Jeffrey L. Buller, PhD, is the director of Leadership and Professional Development Program at Florida Atlantic University and a senior partner in ATLAS: Academic Training, Leadership, and Assessment Services. Buller is the author of more than a dozen books on higher education leadership and over 200 articles, essays, and reviews. His most recent book, Hire the Right Faculty Member Every Time was published by Rowman and Littlefield in 2017. Buller is an expert in providing academic leadership training programs that are enjoyable and immediately practical at colleges and universities around the world.

Edna B. Chun, DM, is chief learning officer with HigherEd Talent. She has more than two decades of strategic human resource and diversity leadership experience in public higher education. Her work and publications focus on academic and administrative talent practices that build organizational capacity. A sought-after keynote speaker and facilitator, Chun is an award-winning author and thought leader.

Alvin Evans serves as higher ed practice leader with HigherEd Talent. With more than 20 years of executive-level experience in complex local education agencies and doctoral-extensive institutions of higher education, he works with organizations interested in developing strategic and cutting-edge organizational capabilities. Evans is recognized by his peers as a thought leader and award-winning author. In addition, he is a frequent contributor to major national educational and diversity publications.

Zach Frank, PT, DPT, MS, CSCS, CEAS, is an assistant professor in the allied health department in School of Applied Studies at Washburn University. Prior to joining Washburn University, he worked as a physical therapist. During this time he supervised multiple outpatient rehab facilities. His scholarly interests include safety and efficacy of strength training programs in adolescents and implementation of lean strategies in clinical settings. Frank got his doctorate in physical therapy from the University of St. Augustine for Health Sciences and MS in health care administration from Marshall University.

Tyler J. Griffin, PhD, is an associate professor in the Department of Ancient Scripture at Brigham Young University. With degrees in electrical engineering and instructional technology, combined with 18 years of professional teaching experience, Griffin has three major focal points in his work: best practices for teaching and learning; best uses of technology to increase learning; and best practices for teacher development. He has also developed two major online training programs that have since grown into robust online learning communities of teachers and students. He is also actively involved in designing and developing 3-D immersive learning environments for his students.

James O. Hammons, PhD, has served as professor of the Graduate Program in higher education leadership at the University of Arkansas at Fayetteville. He is also a member of the Academic Leader editorial advisory board. Since obtaining his PhD at the University of Texas in 1966, he has been a consultant to almost 200 colleges and universities in over forty states and provinces. His work in higher education has varied from teaching, to research, to administration, but the major thrust has been helping colleges and universities more effectively improve the quality of life for those who learn or work there.

Patrick Hughes, PhD, is the assistant professor in School of Criminal Justice and director of M.P.S. in Justice Leadership and Management program at the University of Baltimore. He is a former police officer and remains a police academy instructor. Hughes is the 2013 winner of Alvernia University's Dr. Nan Hamberger Founding Dean's Award. In addition, he was named as one of the Central Pennsylvania Business Journals's 2012 "40 Under Forty" and he is the 2008 recipient of Central Penn College's Todd A. Milano Faculty Excellence Award.

Barbara Kaufman, PhD, president of ROI Consulting Group, Inc., has worked for over 25 years as an executive, educator, and executive coach to help individuals and teams increase their leadership effectiveness and organizational capacity. Kaufman is the 1998 recipient of the prestigious Leadership California Leader award for her program design and board development efforts. Periodically she also serves as an adjunct professor at CGU.

Rob Kelly is a writer/editor for the Department of Human Oncology at the University of Wisconsin School of Medicine and Public Health. He is the former editor of Academic Leader and Online Classroom newsletters. Kelly has a BA in political science/liberal arts from the College of New Jersey and studied journalism at West Virginia University.

Muhammad A. Khan, PhD, is the assistant professor in the Department of Mathematics and Computer Science at the University of Lethbridge. Khan is equally passionate about teaching and have won numerous teaching awards including the University of Calgary Teaching Award, and have more than ten years of experience teaching at various universities around the world. Khan finished his PhD in mathematics at the Department of Mathematics and Statistics, University of Calgary and held an array of prestigious scholarships, including Vanier, Killam and Alberta Innovates Technology Futures Scholarships, during his doctoral studies.

Marissa E. King teaches 5th grade at Tulsa Public Schools (Kendall Whittier Elementary School), Oklahoma. She firmly believes in the power of a 'Do Now' to start the day and wants every student to know the power of writing. Her pedagogy is rooted in the core belief that regardless of grade level, content area, race, or socioeconomic status, every student deserves an excellent education. King is also a 2017 Yale National Fellow.

N. Douglas Lees, PhD, is associate dean for planning and finance and professor of biology in the School Science at Indiana University–Purdue University Indianapolis. More recently, his interests have been directed at higher education change and how that impacts the work of department leadership. He is the author of the book, Chairing Academic Departments: Traditional and Emerging Expectations, 2006. Lees earned his PhD in biological sciences from Northwestern University and BA in biology from Providence College.

Karen Sheriff LeVan, PhD, teaches in the English department at Hesston College in central Kansas. With zeal for writing identity across the lifespan, she currently researches and writes about the struggle for words in the 5th grade classroom, college writing culture, and older adult creative writing groups.

Jennifer Patterson Lorenzetti is managing editor of *Academic Leader: The Newsletter for Academic Deans and Department Chairs.* She is a writer, speaker, higher education consultant, and the owner of Hilltop Communications. She has worked in and written about higher education for more than 20 years and is the author of Lecture Is Not Dead: Ten Tips for Delivering Dynamic Lectures in the College Classroom.

B. Jean Mandernach, PhD, is a professor of psychology and senior research associate in the Center for Cognitive Instruction at Grand Canyon University. Her research focuses on enhancing student learning through assessment and innovative online instructional strategies. In addition, she has interests in examining the perception of online degrees and the development of effective faculty evaluation models.

Henry W. Smorynski, PhD, is a Midland University Leadership Fellow.

Peggy Thelen, PhD, is the professor of education at Alma College. Thelen teaches human growth and development, directs and teaches courses in the Early Childhood Education program, and supervises early childhood student teachers. Thelen believes that it is important to incorporate service learning into the education experience. Several of her courses include a service learning component, which gives education students experiences with families and agencies in local communities. Thelen earned an MA in elementary administration and a PhD from Michigan State University in family and child ecology.

Kayla Waters, PhD, LP, is an associate professor in the department of human services in the School of Applied Studies at Washburn University. Prior to joining Washburn University, she worked as a licensed psychologist. Dr. Waters serves on various committees, including the Institutional Review Board and Graduate Council. She has been a reviewer of presentation proposals for professional conferences. Dr. Waters got her PhD in school psychology from the University of Iowa. She graduated summa cum laude with a BA and BS in psychology from Truman State University.

Maryellen Weimer, PhD, has been the guiding hand and constant voice behind The Teaching Professor newsletter since 1987. She is an award-winning professor emerita of teaching and learning at Penn State Berks and won Penn State's Milton S. Eisenhower award for distinguished teaching in 2005. She has published several books, including Inspired College Teaching: A Career-Long Resource for Professional Growth (Jossey-Bass, 2010).

Jane R. Williams, PhD, is the associate dean for Academic Affairs and Strategic Initiatives at dean's office, associate professor of psychology, and director of Interdisciplinary Studies Program at Indiana University – Purdue University Indianapolis. Her focus of research includes how performance feedback, self-evaluation, and multi-source feedback systems can positively influence employee development.

Additional Resources

If you enjoyed this book, Magna Publications has additional resources for you:

BOOKS

For a full list of books by Magna Publications, please visit:
www.MagnaGroupBooks.com

The Academic Leader's Handbook: A Resource Collection for College Administrators

This resource covers topics that matter most to you as a higher education leader. It explores groundbreaking strategies and tools, influential trends, future challenges, and best practices related to excellence in academic leadership.

Managing Adjunct Faculty: A Resource Collection for Administrators

This invaluable guide offers an extensive review of best practices for managing an adjunct cohort and integrating them more fully into your campus community. Whether you're looking to gain better control over a large adjunct program or seeking to get ahead of the curve on a growing one, you'll find it to be an invaluable resource.

Essential Teaching Principles: A Resource Collection for Adjunct Faculty

If you are an adjunct faculty member, this book serves as a quick and convenient reference for the inevitable challenges of teaching in the classroom or online. It provides a wealth of research-driven and classroom-tested best practices to help you develop the knowledge and skills required to run a successful classroom.

Active Learning: A Practical Guide for College Faculty

Whether you are new to active learning or have some familiarity and want to sharpen your proficiency, you'll find knowledgeable, reliable answers in the pages of this resource. This collection covers fundamental topics pertinent to active learning, discusses common problems, and provides solutions and options.

SUBSCRIPTIONS

Academic Leader Today
www.AcademicLeaderToday.com

The free blog and e-newsletter, *Academic Leader Today*, publishes timely articles written by academic experts. Topics address the challenges, issues, and trends that matter most to academic administrators at post-secondary institutions. Published three times per week, the blog articles help academic administrators set direction, solve problems, and become stronger leaders.

Academic Leader Newsletter
www.AcademicLeaderNewsletter.com

Experienced editors, along with contributors from campuses across the country, examine current trends, challenges, and best practices, helping to advance teaching, scholarship, and service on hundreds of campuses across the country.

20-Minute Mentor Commons
www.20mmCommons.com

20-Minute Mentor Commons gives your entire campus unlimited, on-demand access to a library of Magna's 20-Minute Mentor programs. This resource continues to grow as more programs are added regularly. The programs feature top experts in higher education who are ready to answer pressing questions whenever and wherever your faculty need answers.

Magna Commons
www.MosCommons.com

Magna Commons is an online, cloud-based professional development resource for faculty and academic leaders. With a yearly subscription, your entire campus will have on-demand access to a library of the best Magna Online Seminars. Because all seminars are online, users can access this resource whenever and wherever they are. Watch seminars at home, at work, in a group, on a tablet, or even on a smartphone.

Monday Morning Mentor
www.mondaymorningmentor2018.com

Monday Morning Mentor delivers one of our popular Magna 20-Minute Mentor online programs each week of the school year—16 in the fall, 16 in the spring. On a weekly basis, you'll get quality and convenient answers to common classroom questions. Start every week with dynamic professional development programming for faculty and staff.

CONFERENCES

Leadership in Higher Education Conference
www.LeadershipInHigherEducation.com
This two-and-a-half-day conference explores the groundbreaking strategies, influential trends, and best practices that define effective leadership at the college and university levels today.

The Teaching Professor Annual Conference
www.TeachingProfessor.com
This annual conference provides an opportunity to learn effective pedagogical techniques, hear from leading teaching experts, and interact with colleagues committed to teaching and learning excellence.

Magna Teaching with Technology Conference
www.TeachingwithTechnologyConference.com
This conference presents an unparalleled opportunity for anyone in higher education to develop and hone their understanding of technology and enhance teaching through technology-based tools.

National Conference on Student Leadership
www.NationalConferenceOnStudentLeadership.com
The National Conference on Student Leadership (NCSL) brings together collegiate student leaders and campus professionals to learn effective leadership skills directly from cutting-edge innovators in industry, education, and the nonprofit sector.

93239175R00083

Made in the USA
Lexington, KY
13 July 2018